The Cats
on Hutton Roof

(With apologies to Tennessee Williams)

The Cats
on Hutton Roof

MARILYN EDWARDS

ILLUSTRATED BY
PETER WARNER

Hodder & Stoughton
LONDON SYDNEY AUCKLAND

British Library Cataloguing in Publication Data
A record for this book is available from the British Library

ISBN 0 340 86348 X

Typeset in Goudy by Avon DataSet Ltd,
Bidford-on-Avon, Warwickshire

Printed and bound in Great Britain by
Clays Ltd, St Ives plc, Bungay, Suffolk

The paper used in this book is a natural recyclable product
made from wood grown in sustainable forests.
The hard coverboard is recycled.

Hodder & Stoughton
A Division of Hodder Headline Ltd
338 Euston Road
London NW1 3BH
www.madaboutbooks.com

This book is dedicated

to the villagers of Hutton Roof
who have made us so welcome

and

to the memory of

William Rodney Cotton, 1938–2004
Susan Daly Dugdale, 1952–2003
Wyn Stacpoole, 1916–2003
John Alfred Terraine, 1921–2003

who died during the making of it.

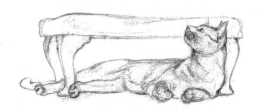

CHAPTER 1

'What do you mean, "he's gone missing"?' Michael is shouting down his mobile phone at me.

'I mean just that. As you know, we got home from Margaret's at around 5.30 and after you all left for the pub I tried to find him, but I've seen neither hide nor hair of him since then and I've no idea how long he'd been gone before that. It's now 7.30 and I'm really worried. Michael, please come home.'

'Can't a man have a pint in peace?' he sighs, but above the hubbub of background conversation and laughter, I can hear in his voice just enough resignation to allow me to relax a little, knowing that soon there will be more hands on deck to start the search in earnest. Shortly after this I hear the front door bang open and in comes Michael, followed immediately by Johnny, his son, and 'big' John, his brother. The cottage is now filled with uncoordinated cries:

'Pushkin, come on, Pushkin.'

'Where are you, boy?'

'Come on out from wherever you are.'

'Come on, you old rascal, come on.'

'Pushie boy, here boy, c'mon.'

'Puss, puss, puss, puss – what a good pussy you are, you are, you are *not*!'

As the volume increases I walk towards the three-man task force with my shoulders shrugged high and my palms upturned in frustrated apology.

'I'm really sorry to drag you back, but I'm at my wits' end. The two girls are curled up asleep on our bed, but I cannot for the life of me imagine where on earth Pushkin can be. I've looked simply everywhere and now I'm beginning to think that he must have got out into the street.'

'You don't really mean that, do you?' Michael grimaces

at me. I see John's eyebrows go up and Johnny starts heading for the door. Out they all troop and I hear their voices fading away into the distance as they dolefully call out 'Pushkin' and variations on the theme of 'come here, cat' and 'you just wait till I get my hands on you'.

Moon Cottage stands on a busy road, and although we had always let our former cats, Septi and Otto, wander the streets freely, since Otto's premature death on the road outside just after her kittens were born, we have contained those same offspring, Fannie and Titus, either inside the cottage or in an enclosed yard in the garden at the back – with forays into the larger garden only under strict supervision. The same restrictions are in force for the currently errant young tomcat, Pushkin, who joined our household just under two years ago and who, in common with all his breed, the Russian Blue, is a sweet-natured but distinctly timid cat who, if suddenly released into a main road without any street wisdom at all, would panic at the first 'whoosh' of an oncoming car. As the voices of the men become indistinguishable I redouble my search round the cottage, becoming increasingly convinced that Pushkin must still be inside but, to my mounting shame, as I call out for the umpteenth time, I hear my own voice starting to crack.

'I simply don't understand how he could've got out. There isn't any way he could have broken out, or rushed between someone's legs without us seeing him,' I hear myself wailing to no one in particular. As I enter our bedroom I look across at the two female cats curled up on our bed, each in her own hollow in the squashy duvet. Fannie, a delicate tabby-tortoiseshell (torbie) with a heart-shaped face, looks up at me, her eyes large with concern at my agitation, and Titus (male name, though a female cat, because I am not very good at sexing them when they are little!), a handsome ginger (red) tabby, also surveys me, but with markedly less interest: she yawns widely and puts her head down again, flipping her tail neatly over her nose. She then lets out a long sigh that shudders through her whole body.

'Yeh, well, I know. It's a hard life and all right for some. Why can't you just tell me where he is? Why? Why? Why?' I admonish, looking down at my watch.

It's 8.30 p.m. I hear the key in the door and go rushing downstairs, but I know from their silent entry that the three men have drawn a blank in their search for Pushkin. John and Johnny settle down to watch television and Michael comes upstairs and puts his arm around me.

'I know this is crazy, but I am convinced he has got himself into a wardrobe or something somewhere and has somehow hanged himself, and we will find him one day by the smell,' I whisper, because it is too awful a thought to express aloud.

'Why hanged, that is the least likely thing to have happened surely? I am more worried that he is just trapped somewhere, but he will come out, or we will hear him, I am sure,' Michael attempts to reassure me. I get a meal together and we eat in mournful silence.

As the 10 o'clock news comes to an end, I slink upstairs to my desk in the bedroom and open up the computer. Settling down intending to read email I try to shift the resisting footstool and, as I look down to determine what's in the way, to my incredulous delight

I see the sleek, muscular, panther-like body of Pushkin, jammed underneath it, fast asleep. After hugging him (and yes, I confess, shouting at him a little too) I break the good news to the menfolk below, and I think they are genuinely pleased he is alive and well – though I get the distinct impression from them that it will be some while before Pushkin going AWOL will be allowed to activate a red alert on this scale again.

It is now early spring, and in the time since Pushkin as a young kitten – he is now just over two years old – swelled the feline ranks to three within Moon Cottage there has been an alliance of sorts, but it is not always a comfortable one. The two sisters, Fannie and Titus – they will be four at the end of April – are very close and spend much time engaged in allogrooming,* which never includes Pushkin. On the other hand, Pushkin is clearly enchanted by Titus, whom he appears to infuriate by his constant shadowing of her every movement. If she wants to eat, then so does he. If she wants to laze on the sofa in the sitting room, then again so does he. If she wants to lie in the tiny rectangular patch of sunlight on the bathroom carpet, then, by golly, so does he. Titus, when Pushkin follows her, could never be said to actively encourage his behaviour. When she is eating and he muscles in, which he routinely does, she sighs; sometimes she clocks him one, gently but crossly, with her front leg, and she has recently developed the habit of filling her mouth with the Hill's dried food (which is all she will eat, rabbit being the preferred flavour) and dropping it a few inches away from the bowl over which Pushkin will now be lording it, so she may eat in peace. Pushkin appears serenely indifferent to the irritation he is causing his beloved, and the fact that Titus gets any space of her own at all is due to the fact

---

* The grooming of each other to mutual advantage.

that Pushkin, sleek, muscled and panther-like though he may appear to be, is also exceptionally slumberous. This trait of his calls to mind the dormouse at the tea-party in *Alice's Adventures in Wonderland*, as he spends at least an equal amount of time as that fabled rodent fast asleep. So at the point when Pushkin naps, then, and only then, is Titus free to wander on her own or to schmooze with her sister.

Pushkin's fondness for Titus appears to be constant and strong, whether Titus is on heat or not. When, however, she is on heat and lies in wait for him in order to 'present' to him, Pushkin is the master of the graceful sidestep and, having circumnavigated the obstruction without a glance, he will then sidle off to another part of the house to lie down and have a long sleep. I have discussed his mystifying reluctance to mate with Titus with our vet on a number of occasions and we are at a loss properly to understand what is the impediment, unless it is that Pushkin is so used to being swiped at by the two queens that he just refuses to believe the invitation is a genuine one when it does come.

When Pushkin first came to us I had hoped that

eventually he might father one litter from one of the two girls, and then I would have them all neutered, but it now appears that this is unlikely to happen, so I frequently agonise as to whether I should neuter them anyway. As a point of interest, Pushkin's behaviour with Fannie is quite different from the way he is with Titus. Most mornings around feeding time he will try to befriend Fannie, but as his initial greeting always comes in the form of a strong head butt (endemic to the breed) which she detests, she invariably hisses back at him, and even Pushkin, who in a touchingly amiable way can be slow on the uptake, recognises that he should venture no further. I find it very sad that Fannie is so standoffish with him, as she must understand that his head butt is meant in friendliness, but her rejection of him never falters. So, having received the ice cold shoulder from Fannie, he tends to skirt round her and, on the whole, he keeps out of her way. Sometimes they will both lie near to, but not touching, each other on a bed, but they will never share a chair. When Fannie is on heat, however, it is another matter. Pushkin is clearly attracted to her in so powerful a way that he overcomes his customary shyness and recurring rampageous pursuits take place. Fannie, unlike Titus, usually refrains from offering herself to him in any form and the chase terminates abruptly with her turning on him to hiss – and sometimes she will finesse this with a slashing of claws; or, and this is the most likely outcome, she will leap up on to the top of a bookcase or wardrobe in which domain she alone remains ascendant, being the most elfin-like of the three cats – a creature of the air – with an inbuilt yearning to climb as high as possible and with a remarkable sense of balance.

So that is the status quo at Moon Cottage at this point. I sometimes wonder reflectively if three in itself is not the problem, but I conclude that whatever awkwardness there is among these cats, it is more likely to be caused by the introduction of a strange male into the midst of a true sorority rather than three as a quantity, and Pushkin is for life, so we will all have to make the best of it!

CHAPTER 2

As I look up from my desk I find myself mesmerised by the tension I see in Fannie, in her body language and her facial expression, as she stares out of the bedroom window, head tilted upwards towards the roof line of the cottage which juts out above her at right angles, where a plump, round woodpigeon is perched on the tiles with its back to us, nonchalantly preening. Initially my attention has been drawn to Fannie by the sinister chattering of her jaws clacking together.* This has now

---

* The tetanic reaction – a rehearsal of the killing-bite. See *Catwatching* by Desmond Morris (Ebury Press, 2002).

stopped. The little cat's eyes are motionless, directed towards the bird in total concentration. Her face whiskers are standing stiffly out and the front few are curling forward in eagerness. Her ears are pointed arrow-like towards her prey, except that every few seconds – and at great speed – they flip back and forth to take soundings. Intermittently her ears quiver, violently. These shivering spasms are almost certainly involuntary, and bewitching in their urgency. The woodpigeon finishes its ablutions, opens its wings, and flies off cumbersomely across the garden. Fannie shifts her gaze to straight ahead, continues to look through the window for a few more seconds, and then casually jumps down.

It is late March and today has been exceptionally warm. The hot sun has rocketed the temperature up and, unusually for Britain at this time of year, the thermometer has registered a sultry 20 degrees Celsius. The whole afternoon long, as the heat has increased, we have been assailed by a series of seemingly unending detonations. The source of these sounds is the large leathery grey pods, hanging down from the boughs of wisteria that embrace three-quarters of the cottage, noisily exploding open to broadcast their pea-like seeds as far out into the garden as a pod can throw. This is an annual phenomenon that generally happens on one afternoon in spring each year, shortly before the new feathery blooms, which in their turn will metamorphose into pods, open to cascade luxuriantly down in those delicate mauve tresses that make them so beloved of English villagefolk up and down the land.

Throughout this hot afternoon the cats have visibly relished it. They have lain, in turn, on the table in their little yard luxuriating in the heat around them. As their fur absorbs the warmth from the rays of the sun their sides move in an almost inaudible purring. From time to time, a tail will twitch slightly in pleasure. There seems to be an understanding between all of them that each may take a go and then retire and another one take its place. As the afternoon gives way to evening, the temperature starts to drop rapidly, and with this drop in temperature the wisteria pods seem to twist and explode even more fiercely than before. This has been the one irritation to the cats throughout this hot interlude and now, with the escalation of explosions, Fannie and Titus are showing increasing restlessness. Pushkin, undoubtedly the most nervous of the three of them, finally gives up – following an especially loud report – and, jumping down from the table, he rushes indoors. Sometimes, it seems, enough is enough.

The following day it is back to the grindstone for Michael and me, and before we leave for work at our customary hour of 6.45 a.m., I ask Michael to put out some rubbish. I am always the last to be ready and it means that Michael has, by default, become the master of the early-morning domestic chores. That evening, as

we enter the cottage at around 8.00 p.m., we are both assailed by a shrill wailing from outside the kitchen door. Only one of the cats has a voice pitched so high.

'I *don't* believe it.

You've shut Fannie out all day!' I whinge, opening the back door to let her in and, hearing the echo of my own voice, now aware that I sound uncannily like Victor Meldrew as I do it. Fannie belts in and races upstairs like a bat out of hell.

'Well, I didn't mean to, and if you got up in time *you* could have thrown the rubbish out, and it wouldn't have happened, so don't blame me!'

'But why didn't you look?'

'She's all right, isn't she?'

'That's not the point, and anyway she might not be. It's a miracle it didn't rain.' By this time, Fannie has come downstairs again and is eating as if she'd been locked out for a week. She avoids all eye contact with both of us, so we know we are in for a spell of aggrieved avoidance, and shortly after this she takes herself upstairs and curls up on top of the bookcase for the night.

Later on that evening, in spite of the tribulations of having accidentally shut Fannie out, we leave the back door of the cottage open into the little yard as it is an unseasonably warm night. We are both sitting, unusually for us, glued to the television watching an old film filled with sentimental associations for us both. It is reaching its most emotionally charged climax when our viewing is rudely interrupted by the spectacle of Titus chasing a small brown mouse straight across the carpet in front of us. The mouse darts round the back of the television and cowers there, in a dark and inaccessible corner. Titus sits squarely and obtrusively in front of the television quivering with predatory interest and causing Michael to say unkind things to – and then about – her. Undeterred, she continues her ostentatious vigil. I try to move the television out of the corner to get at the mouse.

'Please can you help me? If I hold a jug you can chase him into it?' I plead.

'Marilyn, sit down, I really want to watch this film. We can sort the mouse out later.'

'But it might have died of a heart attack by then!' I remonstrate.

Michael mumbles and grumbles, but finally he moves the television and between us we manage to scare the small rodent into a glass jug. Michael takes it out into the garden while I restrain all three cats, who have foregathered for the fun within the kitchen. When he returns to the sitting room where the film is still in full sway, he has a grin from ear to ear.

'You'll never believe what happened when I went to let the mouse out,' he says.

'What happened?' I ask dutifully.

'Well, he just looked up at me, and in a tiny little voice he said "Thank you, Michael, for saving my life".' Michael delivers this last sentence in the highest possible falsetto. I giggle helplessly.

That was the end of March, and it is now late April. We have had a week of almost unending rain, and as a result of this the cats have been pretty solidly contained within the cottage. Over the weekend we have been away, so this morning I open all the doors and windows wide to let in the fresh air and sunlight. There is a strong breeze blowing, almost as if it were still March, but there is glorious bright sunshine, which gladdens the heart and makes the world seem joyful and as if there is just a hint of the promise of summer around the corner. Fannie and Titus gratefully bound outside and leap up on to the large garden table. It is the first time for about three days that they have been properly out in their yard. Pushkin remains firmly asleep upstairs, as is his way. I am at this time still feeding the birds, both on the ground outside the cats' enclosure and also from the hanging feeder, because I am in sympathy with the school of thought that believes that many of the birds who feed their young on worms and insects themselves need seeds and nuts in the breeding season right through to the early summer when seeds are not readily available. The feeder had run out over the weekend and I quickly fill it up. Following this replenishment, today the tally is one erstwhile derided and now rare house sparrow; one robin on his own, but who sometimes allows another one near when he is feeling less belligerent than normal – although on most days he picks a fight with one of the smaller birds, usually a finch; a pair of blackbirds; a pair of dusky pink and grey-collared doves; plump cooing woodpigeons – three for some reason; two completely stunning goldfinches; two redcrests, which are the envy of our friend and cat-sitter, Eve, who, in spite of living in surroundings close to paradise down by her canal, does not have resident redcrests; multiple bluetits; two pairs of chaffinches; two noisy chiffchaffs; and sometimes, but not today, a magnificent bullfinch. As I am idly looking out through the lattice fencework I see the hen blackbird – lighter brown than her larger blacker partner – land on the back of the garden bench that stood for so many years in my father's garden, with her beak crammed full of long trailing grasses. She can barely take off, weighed down as she is by her burden. I watch her flap her wings labouredly, and instinctively I duck as she flies straight towards us, up over the fence of the cats' enclosure where she then lands in a knot of wisteria leaves and branches surrounded by the long pendulous blossoms just above and to the right of the opening of the back door.

Fannie and Titus, who are on the table below, watch her in fascination. Fannie especially is enthralled by the spectacle. Before I can stop her, she has leapt up off the table and sprung up on to the topmost hanging

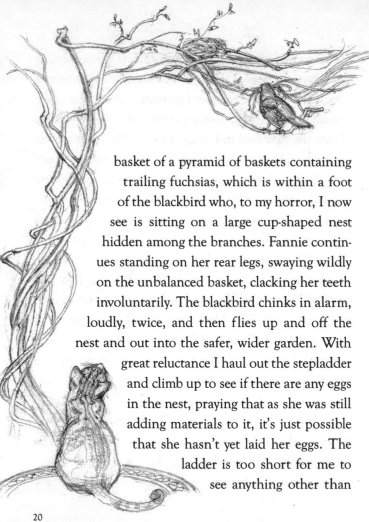

basket of a pyramid of baskets containing
trailing fuchsias, which is within a foot
of the blackbird who, to my horror, I now
see is sitting on a large cup-shaped nest
hidden among the branches. Fannie continues standing on her rear legs, swaying wildly
on the unbalanced basket, clacking her teeth
involuntarily. The blackbird chinks in alarm,
loudly, twice, and then flies up and off the
nest and out into the safer, wider garden. With
great reluctance I haul out the stepladder
and climb up to see if there are any eggs
in the nest, praying that as she was still
adding materials to it, it's just possible
that she hasn't yet laid her eggs. The
ladder is too short for me to
see anything other than

the underside of the nest, but by holding a small looking glass over the top of it, at the full extent of my arm, I establish that it is empty so I gently lift it out and place it in another tangle of wisteria in the outer garden where I hope she may find it. I suspect the truth of the matter is that birds need to select their own sites and are not very happy having these important homemaking decisions made on their behalf. Besides, when I place the nest in its new position, it is merely balanced on the branches and not cemented in by mud, as the birds prefer. This nest was still very damp on its underside where the mud was yet to harden, and she had just finished lining it neatly with the long grasses I had seen her bring to it. The blackbird flies back a couple of times in the next hour and I go out and flap my arms at her and try to scare her off. She is displaying remarkable determination as the cats are clearly in evidence, lounging around on the table outside, but after a further two hours she is no longer visible from my study window, although I can see a male blackbird regularly helping himself to the food supply.

As a cruel paradox, three days later I open the back

door into the cats' yard and find two (not even just one) eggshells of whitey-bluish hue with slight speckles, almost certainly blackbird eggs, which, contents already devoured, I imagine have been dropped by the marauding and dreaded magpies. Magpies are the only birds hereabouts – although crows behave similarly in more open countryside – whose habits regularly induce in me feelings of considerable ill will. I am unable to discern a single attribute of charm they might possess in all their vile carryings-on. They terrorise small birds and kill chicks and eat eggs. They are raucous and have fights with one another when they are not plundering other birds' nests, and the very best that one can say of them is that their striking plumage of black and white gives them a smart and – happily for smaller birds – highly visible appearance, but it is a sight I would gladly forgo. One for sorrow, two for joy, seems to me a serious misrepresentation of how it actually is on the magpie front.

CHAPTER 3

April, with its tortured and shifting weather, has fulfilled its customary role of 'mixing memory and desire, stirring dull roots with spring rain'* and, having finally blustered itself to a close, May has come in full of promise, riding on the back of fresh breezes and bright sparkling sunlight; but perfidy lies around the corner. As I sit tapping at my computer keyboard upstairs I become aware that the sky has darkened mightily and there is an extraordinarily heavy atmosphere. It is clearly

---

* 'The Burial of the Dead' from *The Waste Land* by T. S. Eliot (1922).

going to rain, but as I look up at the sky I am astonished to see a spread of the blackest clouds imaginable stretching as far as the eye can see. Unable to alter anything and feeling safe within the confines of the cottage walls, I shrug philosophically, but by now the wind has got up and the temperature has dropped significantly, so finally I stir myself to close all the windows and put on the heating. I hear a distant roll of thunder, the length of which surprises me. Then suddenly there is a hurling and clattering noise, which is deafening. Hailstones the size of small marbles are smashing to the ground, hitting the garden table and bouncing back up at the windows. A slate from the roof crashes to the ground. There is another crack of thunder and everything is backlit by fierce jagged lightning. I hear distantly the plaintive contralto miaow that is the boy Pushkin's and I go downstairs to find him. It is so dark now, although only mid-afternoon, that I can barely see to walk, and very nearly tread on him because he is crawling along the floor on his stomach, something I have never seen him do before. I pick him up in my arms and cradle him. Further demonstrating his timidity in a way new to me, I feel him go limp with fear as he curls his body into a circle and buries his nose and eyes under his front legs and tries to wriggle his body into my body for protection. Unable to find the sanctuary he is seeking in my arms, with much agitation he scrambles round and leaps down to the floor where he flattens himself and tries to reverse back under the ottoman as far away from the windows and doors as he can. This proves to be so uncomfortable for him that very quickly he crawls back out and squats low on all fours in a hunched-up, miserable heap, eyes alternately staring towards the nearest window at the fearsome noise, or back down at the carpet in front of him with his nose almost on the ground.

I leave him be for the moment, and go in search of the other two cats. I find them walking restlessly from room to room as the bombardment outside continues and, as I watch them and our ears are assailed with yet another deafening rumble of thunder, they instinctively lower their torsos to the ground as they move; as they sidle out of the room, they seem to flow round the

door, rather than actively walk through it. The noise is quite remarkable and the hailstones are now piled high in little white heaps everywhere. Inside the cottage this has produced an instant steaming up of all the windows. The lightning and thunder explode twice more, with a greater pause between the former and the latter as the eye of the storm moves away. And then silence. The blizzard has abated and the clouds start to clear.

I check out the cats and discover Pushkin nestled

down on a pile of blankets on the floor of our huge built-in wardrobe, which is his customary sanctuary, and the two girls are curled around each other on top of our bed. I then go out into the garden. Many of the taller plants are flattened to the ground and I find two pantiles on one of the flowerbeds, one broken and one intact, having been dislodged from the roof by the force of the hailstones. Remarkably, however, the birds have started what sounds exactly like a dawn chorus. Glorious, liquid trillings fill the air. I leave the gate open so the cats can go out, but they stay inside. There are still mounds of frozen ice in little piles everywhere, but as the hailstones melt, the volume of water swilling along the road outside is exceptional, and as I walk back into the cottage the silence is punctuated by the metronomic swish-swish of the rush-hour traffic as it wends its wary way homewards past our front door.

Two days later, on a completely tranquil sunny day which could not be more different from the day of the hailstones, I am sitting quietly at my desk when I hear the most remarkable racket coming from the garden. The bird feeder is hanging from an old-fashioned iron street lamp that we introduced into the garden to use as a garden light, and which is currently missing a screw in its anchorage, so in any wind at all it is rather wobbly. As I look through the window, expecting to see some giant bird attacking the feeder, I am amazed instead to see a large fluffy grey squirrel hanging off the lamp by his back legs in the manner of an experienced trapeze artist, while trying with all his might to extract seeds and nuts from the holes in the feeder with his front paws. His weight hanging from one-half of the crossbar of the lamp is making the whole lamp rock violently. As I watch it swaying noisily from side to side, an especially bold assault from the squirrel makes it lean over at an acute angle. Without thinking, I shout out through the window:

'What the hell do you think you are doing?' I'm completely unable to understand his reply, but reply he does, over his shoulder and chitteringly fast, just before he scarpers over the red brick wall and scrambles up into my neighbour's towering antique pear tree, from which vantage point he continues his muttered insults. I should have realised all along that it was not the delicate finches, or the acrobatic tits, or even the bombastic robin that had previously ripped off the perches, causing all the seeds to fall to the ground, or indeed gnawed through the wooden bars of the lower section that was meant to protect particularly small birds, but altogether a more wily and muscled creature, with an even larger appetite than theirs.

Later on I hear more noises coming from the same direction, but even without looking they clearly stem from an ornithological source. When I do finally look out of the window I see an adult sparrow busily flying back and forth between the feeder and two three-quarter grown chicks who are sitting idly on the bench below, fluttering their wings in that demanding manner young birds have with their hardworking parents. What surprises me is that while I know that adult sparrows will eat seeds, I thought their young would eat only insects, but these two are showing marked vegetarian leanings – or maybe they are just so lazy that they will eat whatever is put into their mouths.

≈

Around this time, we take our annual holiday in France and we leave the cats to the tender and long-suffering mercies of Michael's son, Johnny. When we finally arrive at our haven in Languedoc Roussillon we discover from our hosts, Alan and Valerie, that their cat, Blossom, has died. This hugely saddens me. Blossom was an exceptionally friendly, warm and soft-furred cat who used to keep me sane by furnishing me with a 'cat-fix' in the absence of my own nearest and dearest felines, and who always made it plain that she considered the thick carpet of lush damp periwinkle that covered the terrace of our cottage was in reality hers. She also had pretty much the same perspective on the inside of the house we stayed in, even before Alan and Valerie owned it, but very welcome she was too. This now leaves Alan and Valerie with Erin, their Westie, in sole charge.

As we share a bottle of wine on their terrace, we look out over the central courtyard of the village which is the communal 'garden' shared by all the surrounding houses and which, at different times since Michael and I have been regularly visiting the region, has been seriously overrun with feral cats, several of whom were manifestly brain-damaged. I ask Alan what is the current state of play among the wild cats of the village. He makes me laugh when he outlines a delicious piece of over-zealous feline control, which several local people have unwittingly been orchestrating. There is a new contraceptive pill for cats which is apparently very effective, and it needs to be fed on a regular basis. However, it turns out that several citizens (at least three, says Alan) with a strong sense of social responsibility have been out there putting the same pills into different piles of food, which have no doubt been eaten by the same pack of cats, so it may well be that the female and even the male cats of the village are receiving up to three times the dose they should be getting on any one day.

CHAPTER 4

On our return from holiday, Pushkin retains the disconcerting air of a cat who is not quite sure who we are, exactly as he did last year, when first we enter the house. Who is to say what the short-term memory of a cat might be, although evidence suggests that this amnesia is Pushkin's very own, rather than common to all cats. On the other hand, of course, it may just be his way of putting us down! Fannie assumes a sulk as soon as we walk in through the door, but adorably cannot keep it up for very long, and typically within minutes of our entering the cottage she comes miaowing round to us, tiptoeing sideways and undulating her long upright

tail from side to
side, shivering with
pleasure as she looks
up searchingly into our eyes. I
ache just thinking about her
greeting. Titus is different again.
She lurks outside the nearest
room so she can hear what we
are up to, but will simply not
come in; when she does finally
come in, she jumps on to the back of a sofa or
chair and avoids being touched or picked up by anyone.
If they try to cuddle her she will just jump down and
move into another room. For Titus, if we have been
away for a 'long-haul' holiday, like a fortnight, it will be
a good three days before we are 'forgiven' properly, and
only after this cooling-off period will she be back to
schmoozing and climbing all over us and shedding her
white and ginger hairs so lovingly in her normal cuddly
manner.

~

May has slipped into June and all danger of frosts has now passed. The garden is in its finest livery. Foxgloves in shades of cream and pink and magenta are loftily waving from every bed. The spring rains have made them very tall. That splendid, seemingly eternal flower-carpet generated by the sun and rains of late spring and early summer made up of azure-blue forget-me-nots and slightly darker bluebells has gently faded along with the once majestic heads of the common pink and more singular crimson rhododendrons, and in their place are swaggering lines of pink and red peonies, surrounded by the taller Californian pink poppies and their blousy orange counterparts. Across the lawn in the opposite bed stand proud delphiniums on the edge of opening their blue flowerheads, surrounded by the burgundy, pink and cream spikes of lupins, and at a lower level there are the wild blue geraniums, pale mauve chives, and pink ground roses. The climbing roses are in full flower, rampaging over the wooden frames of the pergola in papery pink and darker burgundian profusion, weaving themselves into a glorious tangle with three different types of honeysuckle, and adding their colour to this amazing palette are the huge saucer-sized blooms from a white and purple clematis intermingled with the more usual mauve variety. Walking under this bower is almost intoxicating as the heavy scent of the honeysuckle merges with the more delicate scent of the roses. In the heat of the June sun the dark shade is sensually welcome.

Geoffrey comes to stay, and he and Michael sneak out into the garden and sit down on Michael's 'secret' bench in one of the honeysuckle tunnels, hidden behind a wall of foxgloves where I cannot see them, drinking wine and beer and laughing conspiratorially, while I clatter pans mildly protestingly in the kitchen. I do not really mind, however, as I know mostly they are talking football, and I will hear the real news when we sit down to eat together.

The garden is more glorious in this month than any other month of the year, and although I cannot take credit for it – it having been designed with care and passion by its former owner some years earlier – I love it and tend it sporadically and wallow in the opulence of it. As we sit down to eat at the table in the cats' yard we look up at Shirley's pear tree standing behind the shared garden wall of the two cottages, which this year is supporting more magnificently than ever before a rampant climbing rose. The rose has wound its way abundantly to the very top of this tall old tree. Shirley tells me that she planted it only seven years ago in a bucket without a bottom at the foot of the thirty-year-old pear tree, and it is called Paul's Himalayan Musk. The pear tree looks like a magnificent rose bush on a scale beyond imagining.

Geoffrey is staying with us for a week while he researches information for a book he is writing, and one evening, shortly after the three of us have returned from our different pursuits in central London and are just beginning to wind down from our day's exertions, I sneakily rush upstairs before anyone else can get there in order to have a quiet few moments on my own. As I open the door into the bathroom, I discover, to my horror, right in the middle of a once white bathmat, a large yellow stain of what, judging by the characteristic pong, must certainly be male feline urine. I inwardly groan, as this is what Michael's old cat Septi started to do when he became ill. Many cat behaviourists will say that cats who have been hitherto completely clean and continent within a household will do this only if something has seriously interfered with their equilibrium. All three of the cats are in good health and are eating without any problems, so I feel I can rule out ill health as the root cause for this deviation, but I am aware that although Pushkin has shown no outward signs of full maturity, at around two and a half years old he is now well into his equivalent of late teens, even early twenties perhaps, and it would not be altogether surprising therefore if something or someone had triggered some need for him to mark his territory more aggressively than is his normal wont. As I quietly remove the offending bathmat with the intention of discreetly putting it through the machine at the hottest possible wash, I wonder if I should not make the long postponed appointment to have him neutered.

I return downstairs to the assembled company and start to prepare the evening meal, and somehow or other in the general conviviality of all that is going on I forget to mention Pushkin's lapse upstairs.

∽

It is now high summer and Titus has been fully on heat for a whole week, and vocal withal, in a sort of grumbly, squawky way rather than calling out, which is more Fannie's line of attack. Titus is being especially insistent this time and keeps trying to wake me up by pulling at my lip with her claw and, although it is hot, the only way I can escape her attentions is to dive under the summer duvet. Tonight I see her go out on to the landing and invite Pushkin to lick her. To my surprise he does, and immediately afterwards he pulls a strange face, and I realise as I watch him it is exactly like watching a wine taster at work. He follows this by turning away from

Titus and sets about grooming his own genitalia with blatant disregard for Titus and obsessive diligence to the job in hand. Titus, abandoned on the corridor, continues to display to no one in particular, but with less and less enthusiasm. I get up and briefly try shutting them both into Johnny's room, as he is away, but soon after that I hear 'digging' under the door. I can guess without incurring any margin of error that it is Pushkin trying for his freedom. I open it up, not least to spare the carpet, and Pushkin belts out and runs downstairs. After a small interval Titus strolls out, yawns widely, and walks into our bedroom, from which vantage point she is all geared up to keep her night-time vigil over me, which she has now developed into a Chinese torture. She sits by my head, gently purring, and I, lulled into a false sense of security, slide towards sleep; but at the very moment before oblivion overtakes me, I become aware, first gently and then more painfully, of her clawful presence as I receive her 'stab, stab, stab' in my upper lip. I am probably being punished for an earlier aberration in my cat care.

At the beginning of the evening I had witnessed a

small tableau involving all three cats each steadfastly doing their own thing. Fannie was on top of the dining room table (I know, I know, *hygiene*, and my long-suffering friends do try to get the cats off the table, but it is a hopeless cause!) gently patting a small roly-poly screwdriver, which – from her perspective, rather enchantingly – kept revolving within its own circumference back to the very place it started from. Pushkin, unaware of Fannie, was just sitting in a corner glaring at the skirting board in a manner that suggested something very interesting was behind it and it would only escape over his dead body. Titus, equally unconscious of the other two, had started a vigorous game all on her own with a biro that I had dropped on the floor by accident, which she kept picking up in her claws, holding it up in the air, and then dropping it again. Because I needed the biro, I rather meanly bent down and picked it up and left her without anything with which to play. Realising I had been a little pre-emptive, I bent back down to see how she had taken it. She was just sitting, under the dining room chair, with her front legs demurely crossed, trying really hard not to look hurt and staring out straight ahead as if that was really why she was there. As I continued to watch her, she finally and very slowly turned her amber eyes on to me, and stared coldly back.

'Oooh, Tites, I'm really sorry. Didn't mean to snatch it back quite like that. Will you forgive me?' She continued to stare, and I couldn't tell whether she felt forgiving or not. Well, the nocturnal stabbing is perhaps my answer.

Pushkin, as well as incessantly head-butting Titus without taking any account of her disgruntled face and forbidding body language, has little or no sense of foreplay with his human companions either. His customary manner of entering a room is to peep quietly round the edge of the door, focus on his chosen object, and then simply run at it and land on it – our bed, my desk, my shoulders – it doesn't matter. He is very agile, so although he does this at speed, usually – unless papers are very delicately balanced – he can do it without upsetting things. Sadly for me, though, Titus has been watching him and now she also leaps up on to my desk as many as two or three times a day and with the same absence of warning. The difference is that she is podgy and clumsy with it, so frequently, when she does this, piles of papers go every which way. It's a salutary lesson to me that in multi-cat households, cats actively and continuously watch and learn from one another, good and bad habits alike.

Today, however, Pushkin excels himself by his absence of inter-feline social skills. As I am making the coffee, I watch him cross the room. He approaches Fannie with an apparent determination and, as he closes in on her, to my disbelief he licks her nose, with some force. Now Fannie cannot be licked by *anyone* without a week's notice, a fact that Pushkin should surely be aware of, and yet he looks utterly dumbfounded when she not only hisses, but also slashes out at him and just misses his nose in return. Having withdrawn, blinking, out of harm's way, he slinks off upstairs for a little sleep.

Only a few days after writing the above, Fannie herself comes into oestrus and although she has visibly mixed emotions about Pushkin, tonight she crosses the bedroom towards the wardrobe from which Pushkin is just emerging. He has just done one of his enormous crocodile yawns, making a loud singsong noise of effort, and as he shuts his mouth I hear his teeth clack together. He saunters out and starts a sensual far-reaching stretch, beginning with his shoulders down, front legs pointing far forward and bum up, and finishing with a flourishing shake of each back leg in turn. Fannie waits for him to finish, and then she moves forward and gently licks his nose. He briefly stares straight ahead, and then puts his nose up in the air and walks off. This little tom will just not change his mood to suit the action; he is, it seems, entirely his own man.

'Oh, Pushkin, are you just going to remain an eternal bachelor boy, is that it?'

CHAPTER 5

It is now late July and Michael has just returned home from hospital where he has undergone a much-needed hip replacement operation. When he is first back in the house he is terrified that one of the cats will somehow get under his crutches and trip him up, but very quickly he becomes adept on the crutches and it is wonderful to watch him regain his confidence. The cats are in fact very gentle with him, and Titus in particular spends much time purrfully squatting on his knee. As I believe totally in the healing power of cats, I can only think the closer they are to him, the better. I know myself without a shadow of a doubt that when I have cuddled any of the cats I am more relaxed, calmer, more able to cope with everything, but for me it is Fannie who has this effect most powerfully, whereas Michael's healer is more probably Titus.

On the subject of healing, I have just received an extraordinarily moving letter from a lady in Finland, whose rescue-kitten Mushu has had a profound effect on her:

I never thought I'd be a cat person, but the moment I laid eyes on this little black kitten, Mushu, it was love at first sight. I suffer from chronic depression and Mushu has helped me a lot. He kisses me when I'm feeling blue, tenderly purrs when I need it, he takes care that I go shopping for food every day, and makes sure I clean our home once a week. All this improvement is because of my beautiful black cat! He has been in my life for almost five years now. Even my therapist agrees with me that it was a wise decision to make. I love Mushu to bits and am eternally grateful to him for choosing me at the rescue centre. I made a promise to take good care of him, but I never dreamt I'd get so much in return.

The moment I read this letter I recall countless occasions when the cats that live with us have helped me through bumpy and sad times. They have an extraordinary power of empathy, and although some people see feline behaviour as 'selfish', I believe, to the contrary, that they are especially tuned in to the tensions and stresses in those with whom they cohabit and for whom they have regard, and that they do have therapeutic strengths.

Returning, however, to the subject of Michael's healing, it progresses well throughout what is becoming a long hot summer, and every morning, day after glorious day, we enjoy a leisurely breakfast outside in the little yard where the cats soak up the sun. One day, as I am savouring the sight of Michael becoming stronger and more relaxed, it gradually dawns on me that he is actually enjoying this recuperation, a lot.

'This is the life,' he grins.

'You're feeling much better now, I can tell.'

'It still hurts, I'm just very brave.'

'I know that.'

'I was only joking – it does hurt a bit, but this style of living is rather wonderful. I somehow thought I would miss work, but d'you know, and this is awful, I don't at all.'

'Oh, you will when you get better.'

'No, do you know, I really don't think I will.'

And so, slowly, with Michael's recuperation begins the nurturing of a seedling that might just grow into our longed-for dream-come-true. I become increasingly excited by the thought that this might lead to the fulfilment of our desires, our precious goal, the nirvana that we have yearned for. From the time that Michael and I first recognised our love for each other, we have had – beyond needing to be with each other as much as possible – one absolute dream: and that is to return to our beloved north of England, our roots, our home, the place where we are both most at ease, where the rhythm is the right rhythm for us. That is not to say that we are not happy in the south of England; we are *very* happy here, but our lives down here are ruled by work and so we are here not by choice, but in order to do the work we do. But, and this is a serious *but*, all his life Michael has been something of a workaholic – me too – and I have always worried what Michael would do if the work-machine was removed from his life. But now, all of a sudden, I find that this beaming, peaceful, relaxed man would take to a life of ease and lack of pressure like a duck to water.

So, between ourselves, we start having angst-ridden conversations about whether and how we could afford it, and in the end the answer is yes – if we sell the cottage for its current market price, if we downscale in our future living, and if we generally draw in our horns, then we can do it. Michael will have his sixtieth birthday later this year, and after that time he can look seriously at giving the long notice that his job requires of him, so possibly by next summer we can think about moving. I keep lapsing into reveries of pure pleasure. It is such a long time to wait, however, a whole year. He laughs, indulgently, as he watches me building a myriad castles in the air. Castles that are filled with gleeful cats jumping in and out of windows on to roads that have no traffic on them, and surrounded by fields and woodlands that contain no dragons. Then he gently warns me:

'Remember that the thing that makes God laugh is people making plans.'

Through the summer Michael becomes stronger and more fit as, being grounded by default, he now walks regularly. Quite early on I discover that these walks are frequently interspersed by small get-togethers with one or more members of his little gang of local chums who are his drinking and football-watching companions. I am by now working back in my office in London and find myself mildly envious of his newly acquired 'domestic bliss', but on the other hand I'm so pleased that his contentment with everything continues and he is not showing the slightest signs of boredom.

August is upon us and the heat is phenomenal. We are letting the cats out into the outer garden more regularly, but cannot leave them unsupervised as they would simply jump over the neighbouring fence and out into the busy road where Otto was killed. But we do try to let them out at least twice a day if possible. Titus, in particular, has suffered from the heat terribly today and has been lying in an uncomfortable-looking heap on the floor. I talk to Margot, my sister, about the problem and she tells me that her friend Jacqueline, who lives in France, regularly wraps her own cats in towels drenched with cold water, so I soak some kitchen towel in cold water and envelop Titus within it. She doesn't like it one bit and protests loudly, but she does seem better afterwards – though I'm not sure she will tolerate it as a regular event. Fannie lies on the bed on her back, panting quietly but unremittingly, although generally during the day she is noticeably livelier than poor old Titus. She is of course much thinner. Pushkin is not eating much, but doesn't show his discomfort as obviously as the two queens. It has been 33 degrees Celsius today in our garden, and that is just too much. They are announcing some absurd temperature in Dubai of around 48 degrees, which is inconceivable to me and is practically off my thermometer, so it can't be real.

As always when the weather is like this, we find we need to water the garden regularly, and as soon as the water starts soaking into the soil enough to bring up any slugs or snails, or indeed enough even to produce the smell of wet earth, it flushes out a small but stalwart group of frogs, some of whom eventually work their way into the cats' yard, to the unutterable delight of its feline incumbents, of course. One such is attempting to make a bid for freedom through the big drain by the back gate. As I walk into the yard I see the rigid backs of Fannie and Titus, who are immobile with tension as they peer at a large brown frog who is unsuccessfully attempting to climb the drainpipe, and at this moment Pushkin, who I assume has just woken up, ambles out and then in turn stiffens, as he smells excitement in the air. Slowly he moves forward to see better where and what the action is, and with that Fannie turns her head a perfect 180° and, peering at him down her spine, withers him with a look that makes me laugh aloud, but it works and Pushkin drops back. The terrible thing I recognise afterwards is that I remember that putting-down look so well from school, and had assumed that it was an exclusive piece of human interchange and not one to be found in the animal kingdom.

Anyway, I spoil the fun for them all by scooping up the unfortunate frog with an empty flowerpot and gently releasing him back into the big garden. Shortly after this, I notice an exchange between Fannie and Titus that leads me to understand yet again that the power of a look, and the tension of eye contact, is of great significance between cats. Fannie is curled up on the sofa, nearly but not quite asleep and half keeping her eye open on all that is around her, as she does. (Michael calls it sneaky, but it is merely her way.) Titus jumps up beside her and quite amiably wanders along to smell her, but something on her back makes Titus sniff longer and more intensively than would be normal. Fannie turns round abruptly and lashes out at Titus, who moves back a little and turns away. A few moments pass and then Fannie puts her paw out towards Titus in what seems to me to be a conciliatory gesture, but Titus immediately lashes out at her. What now happens is that the two of them, both sitting upright, stare at each other, and they hold this intense and unblinking eye contact for at least thirty seconds, possibly longer, before Fannie jumps down and Titus starts to groom herself.

Communication between cats is clearly channelled through all their finely honed senses, through touch, hearing and smell especially; but might their emotions be declared to each other by look, as much or even more than by any other means?

CHAPTER 6

Summer fades into autumn, during which time no fewer than four people who were beloved by us die as a result of a variety of infirmities, but they are not the concern of this book or the cats, except to say that by mid-winter the human inhabitants of Moon Cottage find themselves in something of a shell-shocked condition, wondering when the next onslaught might be. During this time, in part to cheer ourselves up and maybe in part to escape from it all, Michael and I have discussed further our plans of retiring early, and we have agreed that we should put the cottage on the market in early spring, that I should prepare to hand in my notice to my boss at work, and that we should start making the cottage ready to sell from February onwards.

Getting Moon Cottage all set for sale is a major undertaking, and Stephen, the son of our neighbour, Shirley, has kindly offered to carry out all manner of projects that we hope will reinforce the obvious charms of the property. He spends many hours in both the cottage and the garden working on anything and everything that needs his attentions. On one of his visits he is talking to Michael, when Michael, who is wearing a pair of exceptionally heavy boots that he has recently acquired, steps backwards into the dining room and we are all electrified by the sound of a scream at a pitch I have never previously heard. Michael lifts up his foot quickly, but the shriek continues. The source is Fannie, whose tail was right under his great boot and who, in fear and pain as he put his weight down on it, has proceeded to make things worse by yanking it out from under with super-feline strength, in the course of which she has ripped off a substantial section of fur and skin from the top third of it.

Watching an animal in pain is quite terrible and

induces in me a sensation of sickened helplessness of the worst kind. I find myself flapping and fussing as I hear Fannie run round the house, still shouting out in pain. From time to time she stops and hisses, just from the pain of it. She dashes round and then suddenly sits down and frantically licks her vulva. She doesn't yet realise that the pain is deflected and that it is in reality coming from her tail. Michael is distraught and tries to comfort her, but she is beyond consoling at this point. Stephen, with innate tact, beats a retreat and says he will come back another time. On top of all this, fireworks appear to be exploding from all around us – in this part of our county, in spite of our regular complaints to our local councillor, fireworks are detonated from early October until early December and the intermittent explosions are adding to Fannie's distress. The combination of her cries and the fireworks has already sent Pushkin slinking off to find the darkest corner of all within the big fitted wardrobe in our bedroom. I seek out Fannie and try to comfort her, but she will have none of it and eventually, with heavy hearts, Michael and I take ourselves off to bed.

The following day is a full working day and we leave at our customary hour of 6.45 a.m., but that night I manage to get home earlier than my norm of 8.30 p.m. and find that Fannie is still evidently in considerable discomfort. She comes down to the front door to greet me as she hears the key in the lock, but as I open the door, she thrashes her tail, and as she does this the pain makes her hiss repeatedly. She sits down and licks her tail vigorously. I manage to get her on my knee and I gently inspect it. Her incessant lickings have now made it very sore, so I know that the following day will find me making yet another visit to the vet's.

That night, rifling through uncharted sections of the freezer, I find a tray of frozen French snails in garlic butter close to their sell-by date, so I cook the lot of them, but keen though we are, thirty-six snails proves too many for just the two of us, and so I push the uneaten ones, swimming in their lagoon of garlic butter, to one side. After a lapse of about twenty minutes, out of the corner of my eye I suddenly spot Pushkin delicately lapping at the garlic butter with his eyes closed. I mildly admonish him and he stops, but as I return to the table I find him finishing off another couple of snail pockets.

'Pushkin, I didn't know you liked garlic? You'll get indigestion, you'll see!' He looks across at me and rather pointedly licks his lips in relish before jumping gracefully to the floor. As he hits the deck he waves his tail up and down with the pumping action that is common to his breed, shakes each of his back legs in turn, and then slowly saunters towards the chair that Fannie is lying on, from where she is watching him in a pained manner. As he gets to the edge of her chair he lifts up his head and licks her nose enthusiastically. She backs away, but when he continues to lick her she lashes out at him. A sore tail and garlic kisses is a combination of too much pain to take in one go.

'Oh Pushkin, it isn't a turn-on, except to someone else who is eating them too; you have so much to learn,' I murmur to his retreating back.

The following morning we go to the vet's and I am horrified when the vet on duty on this particular day says to me that she thinks that in the worst-case scenario Fannie might need the upper half of her tail amputated.

'She would, after all, be perfectly OK with a shorter tail,' she attempts to console me, when I pull a face – and although I don't say anything, I find I can't bear the idea of Fannie losing her glory; it is one of her special things, her long, bendy, waving tail – she expresses her entire essence by those little flicks of the last three inches of her long tail, first to the left side then to the right as she trots around the place, and when she is being cuddled in the morning her pleasure is conveyed by the minutest twitching of it from side to side. The vet continues her examination of Fannie, during which she advises me that her greatest concern is to stop Fannie licking it, but her tail, while it exists in its entirety, is unusually long, so it's hard to create a collar that would prevent Fannie from managing to reach it. She is dosed up with strong antibiotics and also some anti-inflammatories to try to reduce the soreness, but we both agree that there is nothing we can do to cover the site of the wound that would not be ripped off in three seconds flat. 'Your job is to distract her as much as possible, so that she forgets about her tail!'

And so, for the next two days, Michael and I, and sometimes Johnny too, spend every waking hour that we are at home playing and talking and nursing Fannie until in the end she is begging for release to be allowed some peace and quiet; but, I am happy to report, the vet's ministrations of medicines do the trick and she does leave her tail alone, or enough alone for it to mend slowly and for the spectre of amputation to fade into the distance. (Sometimes, in the dead of night, I hear her licking it, and when I do, I get out of bed to try to distract her.) It is during this time of concern for Fannie that I become aware of exactly how delicate can be the balance of emotions shared between three humans and three cats in one household. It is impossible to explain to Titus, for example, why Fannie is being unceasingly nursed, and one morning Titus comes and wakes me up by quite extraordinarily insistent 'kissing'. She just sits on the pillow and keeps pushing her face into mine and brushing me with her whiskers and breathing at me.

'Tites, I do love you, honest I do.'

Tonight the most extraordinarily haunting autumnal thing has happened and it has given me a strange thrill. It is 11.15 p.m. and wave upon wave of geese are flying overhead. I have lost count of the number of arrow-shaped skeins that have traversed the sky high above the roof of our cottage, and each one has in turn emitted that honking heart-rending cry that only geese make, usually the leader to keep the discipline of the tight formation intact, and on they go, their huge wings making a loud thwacking noise as they carve through the air around them. We are within a quarter of a mile of a series of large disused gravel pits, which over many years have evolved into three large lakes, two of which are used for a variety of water sports, but the third one – the most secluded and deepest of them – is a giant bird reserve and contains the largest nesting heronry in Britain (to the consternation of all the nearby would-be fish-laden pond owners). It is home to many indigenous geese and also, to the irritation of the guardians of the reserve, to the ubiquitous and voraciously hungry Canada geese. At all times of year in the morning and at night, it is common to see two or three skeins flying out and flying back to roost as dusk draws in, and to hear that poignant sound as they call out. But tonight this happening is special and it must be some form of migration on an epic scale; also, they are flying much higher, and away from instead of towards the Aquadrome, where presumably they have been feeding. These birds are going on a much longer journey and there are literally hundreds of them. As I stand out in the garden in the dark, soft wet night, looking up and getting a crick in my neck, I feel a strange pain and sadness for all the animals and humans in the world and for the beginnings and the endings of life and love, and feel overwhelmed by happiness and grief for all that has been, is and will be, and a part of my soul takes flight with the geese.

CHAPTER 7

One of the rewards for me of writing the first two cat books has been receiving a veritable cornucopia of stories within letters, emails and phone calls from people whom I have never met, who have chosen to share with me some of the extraordinary cat experiences they have had themselves, many of which are deeply moving. None more so than that of Padraig, who runs a remarkable website of his own called www.moggies. co.uk. It is a website worthy of thorough investigation by those who are internet oriented and passionate about cats, and which he signs off as 'Moggies – Home of The Online Cat Guide'. It contains information and pictures and stories about cats of interest to cat-lovers every-where. As I started to get to know Padraig better I wanted to know more about the work he does in rescuing cats. From the Midlands, where he lives, this is what he told me:

I take strays in my local area, get them cleaned up, and either find them homes or place them in a local No Kill Shelter. My fastest rescue was a cat that was hanging around outside the backdoor to the flats where I live. He had been there for at least three days before I became aware of him [discovered on security cameras]. I fed him immediately and he scoffed a whole tin of food, it seemed pretty obvious that he had no home or that he had just been dumped. I quickly got him into a cat basket and within minutes one of the flat residents came rushing around the corner to tell me that her daughter wanted a stray cat to care for. Her daughter lived a few streets away, so going from stray to finding a new permanent home took less than five minutes for this lucky feline. So far this year there have been three rescues. We have a tail-less cat that lives wild in our little outback area. Her name is Sootee, her owner died many years ago and Sootee will not live indoors any more, she gets fed and cared for by me and two others who keep a close watch on her, all vet fees are split between the three of us. When it is too cold to be outdoors Sootee will come inside to a ground floor flat, but only while it remains very cold. At present the No Kill Shelter I help at is crying out for potential homes for cats as they have just taken on in one go around twenty-plus older cats whose owner sadly died.

(An update to this, as I write, is that Padraig tells me they have found homes for nearly all of them, and there are now only a few left unhomed.) I quickly discovered from Padraig that he currently shares his life with two cats whom he adores, one called Sassy and the other, his newest addition, Ms Tizzy. Sassy is a beautiful long-haired Norwegian Forest Cat whom Padraig met one day at the No Kill Shelter – a meeting which would never have taken place had he not gone there, following a final and heart-breaking visit to his vet with his much-loved rescue cat, Beauty (whom he always refers to as the Real King of England), who had had to be put down, to donate the redundant renal diet food that had been the mainstay for Beauty.

Sassy, no doubt as a legacy from her harrowing past, was totally terrified of everything and was contained in a large cage on her own, to give her some space to cope with her terrors. Padraig, inevitably, took one look at her and knew that she was the one for him. So home

she came and, after some painstaking cat whispering and encouraging her to climb all over him as he lay on the floor, she finally adopted him graciously and lives with him to this day. He then, this year, introduced Ms Tizzy on to the scene, and Ms Tizzy and Sassy are currently working out fully how to accommodate each other, as is the way of grown cats when first introduced to each other, but Padraig reports that the signs of benign cohabitation are encouraging and getting better by the day. I confess to an especial fondness myself for Ms Tizzy as she looks like a cross between Septi and Fannie, being a short-haired tabby with tuning fork marks above her eyes and the same eyeliner markings round her nose as they have.

But Padraig nearly broke my heart when, on questioning him more about his passion for cats and what had triggered it in the first place, he finally told me the following story:

I was placed in a home for children needing care at the age of three. I found out why many years later . . . but can I just say I have a mental block on the years before the age of five and have no recollection of events before that time.

I always thought I was an orphan, no parents, no brothers and sisters, which was the way it was from the age of three to sixteen. The home I was first sent to was mixed, both girls and boys; it was a very happy time for the next four to five years. Then suddenly I was moved to a boys-only home, and that was a very big shock – and so very different. The home was a large one and didn't have full control over the children in its care. There were over 400 kids between the ages of one and sixteen in this home, and it was run by nuns and priests. It was a very tough home, no niceties like birthday or Christmas presents, just the basics to keep you going. As you can imagine, love and affection were thin on the ground.

Enter Tinkerbell, the cat. This cat was to become my link to sanity in an insane world where I was permanently struggling to make sense of what was going on and fighting to survive. Tinkerbell was a large, fluffy, black and white stray that just wandered into the home one day and sat on my lap. The people responsible for us tried to get rid of her, at which point I raised merry hell. I could be hard to control at the grand old age of five.

Eventually they allowed the cat to come and go as she pleased. Tinkerbell always had meat treats from me whenever we had meat. Other times it would be cheese or cooked bacon, which she loved. There were times when I would sneak out of bed at around two or three in the morning and raid the kitchen just to get a decent titbit for Tinkerbell. Although, if truth be known, she didn't need any food from me, she was an excellent mouser – there was many a time when she would bring prey back in and lie down under my bed for a good feast. I would just lie above her and listen to the crunching sounds of bone cracking followed by loud purrs.

On long walks in the sunny countryside Tinkerbell would accompany me and never once went off on her own. She followed me to school and was always waiting on my return. For some unknown reason, nobody bothered with me when Tinkerbell was around – it was as if they all had been warned by someone not to bother me. Often, she would sleep on top of my bed at night. Always purring and giving me slow blinks. It was wonderful having something to hold on to and to give love to in such a time when these things were thought unnecessary.

Then there came one day when she didn't turn up and I knew instinctively that she would never turn up again. It was probably one of the saddest days of my life. Tinkerbell had been with me for a grand total of ten years. Tinkerbell gave a great deal of love and affection; without her, I do not think I would be the person I am today.

When I was sixteen, I was visited by my so-called father, who decided I needed to come home, as I was now able to work for a wage. I found out that not only did I have parents, I also had eleven brothers and sisters, but by that time it was far too late. Unless you are brought up with siblings, it is almost impossible to accept them as brothers and sisters. I was so different from all of them that it was necessary for me to make my own way in the world without this newly discovered family. I have never regretted walking out on my own, as they were far too argumentative and selfish.

All in all, I was the lucky one; I had an upbringing that taught me a great deal about love and respect, and that by a single cat. Something my brothers and sisters didn't have and, as it turned out, never would have.

Because of Tinkerbell I have become a spiritual person (not in a religious way) with strongly held personal ethics, and I don't need to seek the so-called material things in life. I don't look back with sadness at my upbringing; more I celebrate what I succeeded in coming through and surviving. But it was done because of the help of

Tinkerbell, a very fluffy black and white stray moggy cat who gave to me and received back from me love.

I asked Padraig a little more about his oblique reference to the way everyone left him alone when Tinkerbell was around 'as if they had all been warned by someone not to bother me', and he only slightly less enigmatically told me that he thought one of the priests in residence was protecting him, so be it, and thank goodness for it or for him.

I feel sure from having spoken and written to Padraig that he is indeed in some way a blessed person who has gained huge inner strengths from his hard times, and this is in many ways reflected on his website which was first launched in 1999 and now receives one and a half million visits a month.

CHAPTER 8

The new year dawns and with it much excitement within Moon Cottage. I have tendered my resignation at work, and so now there is no turning back. Following the heartache we all suffered from those deaths last year, it is with huge joy that Michael and I now look forward to the birth of his first grandchild this spring and we are thrilled to hear from Damian (Michael's firstborn) and Jo (his partner) that they will return shortly to England and the birth will be here. This morning on the radio a foreign correspondent recalls the words of a Hungarian grandmother as she looks down at her newly born grandson, holding out his tiny hands like a small starfish: 'They bring their own love with them.' Oh yes, indeed they do.

~

One night in mid-January I am awoken by a loud crashing noise. I get out of bed sleepily, and as I turn into the landing to climb down the steep staircase a bitterly cold draught of air bites at my ankles. At the bottom I find Titus looking discomfited and limping slightly, so I conclude she has fallen off some high surface. She is the least nimble of the three of them and the most likely to fall clumsily. In the morning when I let the cats out into the garden I take a careful note of Titus, and she is clearly still lame. Everywhere is white with an iron-hard frost, and as she puts her foot down to the cold ground she tenses up and, as I watch her, to my horror her right hind leg shoots out of joint and sticks out at an unnatural angle to the side and I realise that she is displaying the identical symptoms to those that affected her left hind leg just over two years ago. I shudder, and then find myself denying it is happening. I omit to mention it to Michael.

Two days later it happens all over again, and this time Michael is in the kitchen. I make him watch her and he grimly nods his assent.

'Sorry to say it, Marilyn, but it looks like the same trouble all over again to me.'

'I can't bear it. That operation for a luxating patella is so awful. She hated it and it is so confining and the ongoing pain is beastly.'

'Can you live knowing that she is in that amount of pain now, though, and that untreated it won't get any better?'

'I'll just wait a couple more days to see what happens.'

He shrugs resignedly and I know that he's right, but the longer I put off taking her to a vet, the better it feels to me. But of course that isn't the case because it just nags away at me, worrying me. Three days later finally finds us in the vet's, and after a couple of visits to and fro we are eventually seen by the senior partner, who quickly recognises it as a luxating patella (dislocating kneecap, more common in dogs than cats). Knowing how much I want to avoid surgery for Titus, the vet tries pain relief for some weeks to see if it will help, but

I am finally compelled to go back to her and admit defeat. She then informs me that Titus will need to be referred to a specialist for surgery. When I question that, as the last time Titus had to undergo the op it was done in this surgery, she explains that at that time she had an Australian locum *in situ* who was experienced in the procedure, but this time it really does need a specialist to do it. So the poor little mite is booked in for surgery at a far distant place at the other end of the county, and it is all to happen immediately after I stop working.

Meanwhile we start in earnest with the painstaking work of preparing the cottage for sale. The bulk of the work is being done by the ever-helpful Stephen from next door, who loves nothing better than getting stuck into projects that involve renovating historic buildings. Together we look at the whole of Moon Cottage, inside and out, including the garden, to assess what requires Stephen's attentions most pressingly. There is assorted carpentry and weeding and plastering, but the main thrust of the work to be done is painting. Stephen is one of the most meticulous workers I have ever watched in action, and although I too love things to be done well, I know that I sadly lack his almost obsessive fastidiousness. Like a mantra, Stephen repeats to me: 'It's all in the preparation, Marilyn, everything's in the prep.'

So slowly Moon Cottage begins to glow under the blush of her new clean mantle and I feel ashamed as I realise how grimy we have let the walls become in the years that we have lived here. Michael and I, separately and together over many years, have collected a phenomenal number of books and we decide that we must now take the decision to de-clutter and store as many of them as possible elsewhere, so we start to box them up. As we do a rough 'stocktake' we realise we have over 3,000 books in this little cottage, and further 'culling' is out of the question for both of us as we feel we have already jettisoned more than we can bear. We find an accommodating local firm who agrees to store the books for us and suddenly we see walls where we had forgotten they existed.

On the days that I am at home I am so used to Stephen being part of the woodwork that it seems odd when he is not present in Moon Cottage, and he begins to know every nook and cranny of this cottage as well as he knows his own next door. One day he and Shirley come to us together and suggest that it would be really interesting to have a historical adviser properly date the cottages, as when they were certified as Grade II Listed Buildings they were nominally entered as seventeenth century. Stephen, though, is convinced that they are older than that, so we all agree and a consultant on historic buildings, called Adrian Gibson, who specialises in timber-framed structures, is duly commissioned.

On the day that Adrian and his wife, who assists him in his specialisation, come to the cottage I am writing, and so I leave Stephen to show him round before taking them into his own cottage. My curiosity, however, is whetted beyond endurance – that is to say, I can no longer sit still at my keyboard, when I hear both him and his wife emitting high-pitched squeals of pleasure and excitement, and I trot out on to the landing to see what the fuss is about. He explains that many different features, including the marks on the large beam on the upper landing, indicate to him that without any doubt the building is late sixteenth century, but there are other factors too that thrill them both. He believes that the two cottages were originally agricultural in nature and were one building, probably used for the storing of sheaves of corn, and that around the year 1700 bricks were added on to the wattle and daub as a cladding to the timber frame, which is when the cottages became two, and became fully residential dwellings rather than mainly agricultural. In the report he sends us afterwards he says:

In Moon Cottage bold carpenters' assembly marks are visible, cut by a carpenter's scribe or race knife. These are of medieval rather than post-medieval type.

And then later on he says:

This joint is typical of fifteenth-century and sixteenth-century work, but tends to be made shorter in the later sixteenth century. Everything being considered, this is probably the date of the timber framing.

It is probably the case, in fact, that these cottages are either the oldest buildings, or the second oldest buildings, in this entire area.

As I absorb this information my eyes fill up in wonder. We are living in a building that, because he reckons the date of its erection was around 1570, was built before Shakespeare wrote his first play; built two years before John Donne and Ben Jonson were born; built seventeen years before the execution of Mary Queen of Scots and eighteen years before the defeat of the Armada.

That night, Michael and I open a bottle of wine and ponder on all that we have learnt about the cottage's long life.

'Why are we leaving? We both love it here so much, and now it is even more remarkable than we ever realised?'

'Michael, don't have second thoughts now!'

'Not second thoughts, but it is wonderful here. You love it, you said so yourself. You said you have never been in a warmer, cosier, happier house.'

'I know, but you, as much as me, want to go home, to the North, don't you?'

'Yes, don't worry. Of course I do, we both do. But if *only* we could take this cottage with us.'

'Oh that's the agony. Now you're talking. If we could do that then we would, 'cept it would leave Shirley and Stephen and Karen needing a new east wall and feeling a bit exposed.' Johnny, who has sat down at the table with us at this point, adds:

'But hey, it would give them a huge garden – worth the hassle!'

And then, one day while we are still in the month of January, I receive a transatlantic phone call from my sister, Judy, which fills me with foreboding. Rod, my brother-in-law (and my second cousin, so also a friend from my childhood), has been diagnosed with a rare cancer and, having had one investigative operation, is to undergo further urgent surgery. So already this joyful new year threatens to turn into something completely other.

CHAPTER 9

LOST DOG
At Bishops Wood
Friday 6th Feb, 12 midday

Brindle brown Boxer/Staff
cross – white front paws
Answers to 'SOCKS'

Please help us find him, we
love him & we live in
Maidenhead so he won't find
his way home.

£100 REWARD

This notice appears under the windscreen wipers of every car in the small town and surrounding villages near Moon Cottage on the Sunday following Friday, 6 February. I have it sitting on my desk for ten days when finally I can't bear it any longer and I pick up the phone and dial one of the three telephone numbers on the bottom, and find myself speaking to, as it turns out, the owner of the missing dog. I haven't, of course, found the dog Socks; I am simply in an agony of suspense, and that melancholy Eeyore-like tendency to which I'm prone leads me to assume the worst will have happened and the dog will not have been found, and all will be doom and gloom – and yet, and yet? Anyway, I have an overwhelming need to know one way or the other.

Socks *has* been found, after an interval of just over a week but, interestingly, nowhere close to this part of Hertfordshire, but instead in Harrow, approximately ten miles south-east of Bishops Wood. The man I speak to had put posters up on every telegraph pole and every telephone box within a five-mile radius of Bishops Wood, where the dog had first gone missing;

and, from his conversations with the person who reintroduced him to Socks, he has pieced together a story where he reckons some kids had found a friendly but ownerless dog (he had slipped his collar when he had gone missing) and had taken him off home with them. They then got bored with him and he landed up with the son of the man in Harrow, who took pity on him and was going to give him a temporary home until he could find out where he had come from. Where Socks was remarkably lucky was that the man who lived in Harrow, whose son had brought him home, was driving – unusually for him – close to Bishops Wood, and because he had already passed two telegraph poles in succession with a large printed sign saying 'LOST DOG' his own curiosity made him stop, as he wondered if it might conceivably refer to the dog he was caring for. The odds must have been hugely against the sign being about the same dog, but because it was, the end of this story is a happy one, with dog and owner reunited. I record this story because again and again I hear about people who have gone to extraordinary lengths to find lost animals, and so many times their energies pay off; but I recognise in myself that tendency to just give up too easily and assume the worst (I suspect it is a form of pain sublimation), and the lesson I need to learn is that having courage and perseverance pays off.

The pain of losing a beloved animal and not knowing what may have happened to it is indescribable and can only be fully appreciated by those who have suffered such a loss. One day I am sitting with Judith, my friend and publisher, in her London house, admiring her two strikingly handsome Burmese cats, Daisy and Freda, when we start talking about the agony of cats going missing. Judith, although she lives in London, has the unusual luxury of being able to allow her cats to come and go freely through their cat flap as her house backs on to a series of other houses and gardens, with no roads intervening, as is the way with some residential areas in big cities; Judith does, however, curtail their wanderings after dark. Interestingly, many cat behaviourists recommend the closing of cat flaps at night, regardless of location, 'to protect the cat from cars and creatures of the night and to protect small mammals from the cat at dawn and dusk'.* Indeed, as we are talking Judith says how she always feels more relaxed in winter, because the cats are instinctively happier to have their movements restricted by both darkness and the weather, and when they are safely within, then no terrible things will happen to them.

Judith's most terrible moment with this particular pair was when they were about two years old. One hot summer's night, while she had been entertaining friends outside, she had been aware of the two cats being around in that lovely companionable way they have, and the door had remained open as the twilight had lingered on. As she started to clear up following her guests' departures, she called the cats to come inside. After a small delay Daisy appeared, but there was no sign at all of her sister, Freda. Judith started to call repeatedly from the garden and became increasingly 'paralysed with fear and despair'. At around 4 a.m., unable to sleep and distraught with anxiety, Judith left the house and walked round the streets, calling Freda

---

* *What Cats Want* by Claire Bessant (Metro Publishing 2002).

by name, but there was no response of any kind. She returned to the house, beside herself with concern and worry.

As dawn broke, a long-suffering friend who was staying the night, hearing Judith's repeated calls to Freda, tried to persuade her to go to bed and to simply leave the cat flap open on the grounds that the wayward Freda would no doubt return when she was ready. In spite of this advice, Judith, sick with worry, was still unable even to attempt sleep and it was at this point that she recognises how immensely important her friend was to her, as she simply sat her down and told her what to do, and Judith meekly obeyed. Judith thinks that it helped too that her friend was completely unemotional, and just totally practical about the cat being missing. She said 'write a note on your computer, print it off and take it round', and so she did:

My neutered chocolate Burmese cat, Freda, did not come home last night. She may have got trapped in a garden shed. Could you please check in sheds and garages for me, thank you.

Judith then added her landline and her mobile telephone number, printed the notes out in quantity, cut them up, and started to deliver them around the neighbourhood from house to house; by 8 a.m. she had completed her task.

'The exercise was cathartic, and it made me feel that I was doing something practical to help. But I experienced all those emotions of pain, anger, irritation, despair and pessimism as to whether this would be any use that seize you when something like this happens and you can only wait.'

The hardest thing in this situation is to stop the imagination working overtime, and the most horrific possibilities, which are almost unthinkable, appear in the mind's eye. For Judith the agony was made more acute because as the cats were chipped, and therefore wore no collars, anyone finding Freda would, with the best will in the world, have problems establishing quickly how they might track down the human companion belonging to the cat, as with chipping you have to get the cat scanned at a vet's. Added to which Freda is a beautiful chocolate seal point Burmese, and very 'steal-able', and all this is taking place in London, with its big-city anonymity.

'So what happened next?' I ask.

'Well, within an hour of distributing the leaflets Freda just sauntered in, but very hungry. Although, to be honest, it wasn't really sauntering, more galloping up the path. I do believe, although I will never know for sure, that my note through those doors did encourage someone, somewhere, who had unknowingly shut her in, to make the effort to find her and then let her out – perhaps because of the note, or maybe because they just found her. Being out all night is completely out of character for both of my cats, so I have no doubt that she was locked in somewhere.'

As an aside to this story there is also the question of the reaction of the cat who stays at home. Judith says that Daisy was completely laid back about Freda's disappearance and stayed with Judith in the garden for all those hours out of companionship rather than concern, but would this have remained the case if something either serious or long term had happened to Freda? Do cats know when their close companion is truly in trouble?

The overall lesson for me in this story is that, for Judith, writing that note and distributing it around helped her considerably at the time, as it relieved the complete sense of helplessness she otherwise felt, as it also did for the man with the dog from Maidenhead. And in both cases it may well have been the catalyst for the animal's return.

There are other ways of finding your cat too, such as simply to go out and look for him, but the trouble is that it can also be a recipe for despair when it resembles too closely a search for the proverbial needle-in-a-haystack as it did initially for Judith, and yet, sometimes, it gets results.

It was a January night and Willow (my Tonkinese) had been out all evening. He is a great hunter and there are many months in the year when he dines regularly on rabbit. (I have even known him eat two in a day!) At this particular time he had also been catching the occasional rat, but only as a trophy, not for consumption, but I should have been more curious about where he was finding them! On the night in question I was worried that I had not seen him on my return from work, but comforted myself that whatever happened he was always in by midnight and then the door would be locked . . . but on this occasion 1 a.m. came and then 2 and then 3. By the time morning dawned, I was exhausted and seriously concerned. I dressed, determined to find him.

Jo, whose story this is, met Peter (the illustrator of this book and the previous ones) and me at Peter's local bookshop in Surrey, and talked a little of Willow to us then. Later on, I learnt more. Jo lives in a remote, rural cul-de-sac, with a fair-sized garden, and beyond that there is a large field owned by Surrey Wildlife – so a veritable heaven for an inquisitive cat – and beyond that, even more superbly from his point of view, a yard that's ostensible reason for being was for lorries to service the M25, but that was populated with outhouses and trailers stuffed with things irresistible to rats.

'The best I could do,' said Jo, 'after calling Willow endlessly, was to take a picture of him to the gritting yard. The site had a security office and I pleaded with the lady officer to ask the drivers if they had seen my cat.' Jo, unable to postpone going to work any longer, then departed with her heart in her mouth. She managed, however, to return from her place of employment at 2 p.m. in order to search for Willow in what remained of the winter daylight. She set about searching every nearby pond and waterway and all the cross-field footpaths, calling for Willow repeatedly, but to no avail. She arrived home, frustrated and distressed, just as it was beginning to get dark. As she went into the house she noticed an answer-phone message on her telephone. It was from a driver in the yard announcing, somewhat cryptically, that he had seen her cat; he then left his contact number.

Unhappily for Jo, though, when she phoned him back she discovered that he had indeed seen her cat, but this was when he had been emptying his huge container lorry, which had been parked overnight behind her house, at the Household Waste and Recycling Site in Caterham, some five miles distant from Jo's home and, perilously, over the other side of the M25. As the driver had opened the small trap door at the lorry's base, a terrified cat, resembling the photo he had been shown, had run out and disappeared into the middle of a town that he had never been to in his life.

'Horrified, I panicked and ran out into my driveway, not knowing what to do. I beseeched my new neighbours to help me.' Luckily for Jo, these neighbours, Denis and Hilda, had lived in Caterham until six months ago and knew it well.

'Denis said "Get your coat", and in the dark we set off for Caterham. For two hours we searched the high street and back streets, we knocked on doors, nursing homes, and even the vet's – and at one stage we even went into a pub where I spotted another neighbour of mine who has four cats of his own. I cried out "I've lost my baby" and the other drinkers looked up, aghast, as only my neighbour knew I was referring to a four-legged one. Eventually, after two hours, broken-hearted, I said we should search no more. Denis, however, knowing the town so well, said there was one more place he wanted to look, and so we set off down one more alleyway . . . and then, *I heard him*! As you will know, Tonkinese, being part Burmese and part Siamese, have a distinctive cry, and there he was, cowering in a hedgerow. I grabbed him and stuffed him up my jumper, and between us we got him into the car and drove home. When we finally got home, he did the biggest wee you ever did see! When they are frightened and away from home, cats simply stop going – and he had been missing for twenty-four hours!'

When Jo got back into her house she started the happy

business of phoning the important people in her life whom she had earlier alerted to Willow's absence, and while she was doing this the doorbell rang: and there was her neighbour (the one in the pub) and his daughter, with a fistful of handwritten notices that they had specially prepared for her to take to all the shops in Caterham. Never has Jo been happier to present to anyone the physical presence of why that would no longer be necessary than at the moment she pointed down to her boy, Willow, happily purring by his familiar hearth.

In a postscript, Jo adds: 'I am pleased to say we now have new contractors on that site and the waste lorries are no more, and likewise Willow has brought home no more rats. We also have Golly [a beautiful jet-black glossy cat], who keeps us all sane – he is, however, a real wuss, who prefers to stay well within the boundaries of house and garden, and whose only failing is to destroy all the carpets!' With Willow around, she needs a Golly in her life, it seems to me.

CHAPTER 10

The day of the dreaded operation for Titus has now arrived, and I pack her up into her cat cage, having yesterday starved all three cats of food from the early evening, to their complete disgust, and the two of us set sail – that is to say, we swell the ranks of the early morning commuters jamming up the M1 – for the distant veterinary hospital. I have the wire cat cage strapped in firmly next to me on the passenger seat, with the forlorn figure of Titus within. She miaows briefly and then hunches up despondently, and stares downwards with her nose touching the bedding. Titus is always the least complaining of the cats, the most

friendly, the calmest, and she is also the only one of the
three to whom these awful operations seem to happen.

'I know, it just ain't fair, Tites, and I'm really sorry –
it's always you, babe.' She stares up at me unhappily,
but also with an expression that looks like trust on her
face. I feebly poke my fingers through her cage to try to
touch her, and so reassure her *and* me. The journey
goes on and on, and the last part of it after we leave the
motorway is long and winding and she begins to retch
from carsickness; and as we turn into the car park, she
finally vomits in a watery sort of way. As we enter the
hospital it is still early morning, but it already feels as if
the day is half over.

The vet who is to do the operation, Rob, is charming,
absurdly young, outrageously good-looking and, I am
fervently praying, a skilful surgeon. He is articulate and
patient and I appreciate the amount of time he gives to
Titus to watch her walk about his room and demon-
strate her gait. He seems to be at ease with cats, which
is a big plus. However, as he explains things to me,
using a skeletal model that somewhat disarmingly has a
vital piece of bone missing, for his demo of what will

happen in surgery, I suddenly begin to have the most awful doubts as to why we are here and wonder if I might be guilty of attempting to inflict Munchausen syndrome by proxy* on her, or something akin. Does she really need this operation, I wonder, and although I know that I really shouldn't be asking him this question at this ridiculously late stage, I suddenly hear myself saying:

'I do understand what you have said, but tell me honestly, is this operation really necessary?'

At this point I have the consent form in front of me unsigned and the pen is in my hand. He looks across his desk at me long and hard and draws his fingertips together.

'Her left leg is still coming out and it could originally have been worse than her right leg, and we should possibly consider further surgery on it; but her right leg

---

* MSBP is attention-seeking behaviour by the owner of a pet (or, more usually, parent of a child), manifested by the repeated fabrication or exaggeration of health problems in that pet, generating unnecessary medical interventions and/or procedures on the pet as a result.

must be done. I am sure of it. From my examination of her I would say it is a luxating patella Grade II. I will have to deepen the groove and I may also need to tighten the tissues.'

'Rob, the aftercare and long containment is terrible. If she were your cat, would you have this operation done?' There is a pause long enough for my heart to miss a beat, and then:

'I hate being asked that question,' he laughs. 'But yes, if this were my cat, I would definitely want the problem to be corrected.'

'I'm sorry, I'm sorry. Please do it,' I hear myself mumbling as I sign the paper. Titus just stares straight ahead. Soon after this I leave, having watched Rob carry Titus off in her cage down a long, long corridor. My intention is to collect her either the next day or the day after that, at any rate as soon as she is allowed out.

After I return home alone, I experience that bleak sadness tinged with guilt that is endemic to the hospital visitor able to walk free. Shortly after I get back, at around four o'clock in the afternoon, Fannie lets out a small squawk, and I am so galvanised by her utterance that I phone the hospital. They tell me that they have just this minute taken Titus down to surgery for preoperative investigations. At 5.40 p.m. exactly, Fannie, who is on the bed behind me, screeches out really loudly, and then jumps up on to my lap to be comforted. I know I have to wait for the phone call, so I just stroke her and pray. At 6.30 Rob, the surgeon, phones me and I ask him:

'What exactly were you doing at 5.40?'

'Oh, manipulating Titus's leg to see how bad it really was', he replies. So Fannie's telepathy was not for Titus's safety, but in reaction to her comfort, or lack of it – if, indeed, that is what it was. Anyway, the operation has been performed, Titus has regained consciousness and is now sedated, and they are keeping her pain under control, and as for the rest, time will tell.

In the two days that Titus is at her special referral centre, Fannie in particular is rendered wholly distraught by her absence. I can hardly bring myself to look at her face. It is showing utter, naked grief, and Pushkin too looks most discomfited. They are both restless and walk around the house endlessly. So Titus, the great bonder, whose many talents may well go unrecognised by some, if not all of us, we badly want you home. I cannot wait to collect her, for all our sakes.

When I make the return journey with a light heart to collect Titus, I discover from Rob that she has undergone 'sulcoplasty and tibial tuberosity transportation and lateral imbrocation of the right patella'. He is happy with the changes he has made to the alignment of her leg and expects her recovery to be a good one. I am given a piece of paper by the hospital, which reads:

- Titus needs pen confinement for a further six weeks.
- Supervised exercise but confined to one room.
- Suture removal in ten to fourteen days' time at your own veterinary surgery.
- Return here in six weeks with a view to examining the other leg for surgery.

When I get Titus back – with her right leg four-fifths shaved (the only fur remaining on her leg being a white sock topped by a small ginger frill at the very bottom, making her look poodle-like), so her skin is exposed, naked, from her lower joint right up to her belly, and on her upper flank up to her spine with a long deep sutured scar dissecting the front of the top half of her leg – her would-be-euphoric homecoming is marred by Fannie's absolute rejection of her. One sniff at that anaesthetic-laden breath and the erstwhile grieving sister turns into a scolding dragon. Fannie spits and hisses and carries on as if the devil himself was in the cage in front of her, and Titus sinks to the ground, dejected and in pain and looking more miserable than I ever remember seeing her. Michael shouts at Fannie for being awful. I shout at Michael for shouting at Fannie, because Fannie doesn't understand, and Michael shouts back at me, saying neither does he! Pushkin runs away and hides.

On our behalf, Shirley from next door has borrowed a metal fold-down puppy cage from her friend Cindy, and to begin with we put the cage on the coffee table in the sitting room, near to the log fire, but after Fannie's disgraceful behaviour we realise that Titus needs quiet and rest so we take it up to our bedroom. From then on I spend as much time as I can with Titus in the peace of that room, which in any case is my study. After two and a half days, Fannie finally stops hissing at Titus on entering the room. Pushkin, on the other hand, has at no point hissed at her, although he does sniff at her as if she is altogether a different cat from his best buddy. He often sits outside her cage and just stares at her. Titus hates this, so I have rigged up a blanket as a partial curtain to block out staring cats and also draughts, so if she wants privacy she has it. She has to spend the majority of each day in the puppy cage, so to give her more room I have fixed on to the end of it another cat cage in which she has her litter tray. I have purchased a large squashy dog duvet for her to lie on and, under Rob's strict instructions, I take her out of her cage three or four times a day for restricted exercise (no jumping whatsoever – and that is something of a challenge, I have to say), and also for much needed cuddling and stroking. Whenever I take Titus out of the cage both Fannie and Pushkin immediately climb inside it themselves and eat her food, use her litter tray, and lounge around on her duvet, clearly trying to work out why on earth she chooses to spend so much time in there. Fannie has become amazingly sneaky at stealing the food out of the bowl I have in the cage for Titus, even when the cage is closed, and it becomes increasingly difficult to stop her from hooking her paw in and fishing out food, which anyway is freely available to her at all times down in the kitchen. I put books and small pieces of cardboard to prevent the theft, but still she continues.

The regime for Titus' recovery must include this restricted exercise (which is different from my instructions following her previous operation, when I was told she must be contained at all times, except for cuddling), and also Rob agrees that her morale needs consoling and we should all spend as much time stroking her and talking to her as possible. To this end, as well as taking her on my knee as often as I can, which she does seem to love as she purrs deeply while there, I also let her and Fannie lie together on the bed, and sometimes Fannie grooms her and is surprisingly good at avoiding her operation scar; it seems the bonding is good for the pair of them. This is, however, slightly fraught with danger as it is absolutely essential that at no point does Titus get up and jump to the floor. I find that I can sit at my keyboard with a mirror rigged up so that I can watch the two of them like a hawk, wherever they are on the bed behind me. As I sit there, anxious in case I am unable to cross the room fast enough to stop Titus jumping down from the bed, I suddenly recall with awful clarity:

> She left the web, she left the loom,
> She made three paces through the room

followed, with unseemly haste, by the dreadful:

> The mirror crack'd from side to side;
> 'The curse is come upon me,' cried
> The Lady of Shalott*

---

* From 'The Lady of Shalott' by Lord Alfred Tennyson.

(And oh how we girls giggled when, as eleven years old at school, we were learning that line!) But there are some really bad days in the long process of recovery. Sometimes Titus seems almost comatose with pain and/or boredom and I am at a loss to know how to make her more comfortable. What she wants, of course, is her freedom, and she looks up at me out of her cage with a yearning in her big eyes that breaks my heart. When I try to get her to exercise she is clearly in a great deal of discomfort, and I know well exactly how tolerant cats are of pain so I begin to wonder just how much pain it is fair for her to take. Added to this, Michael is beginning to lose patience with Fannie, and I too am having problems concerning her demands. Fannie is finding what she sees as an unnecessary amount of attention being devoted to Titus as unfair and uncalled-for. However, in her prison cell Titus watches everything and she makes it abundantly clear to Michael and me that she is hungry, nay starving, for love. And so the long days creep by, and if the time drags in this way to a human witness, I dread to imagine how long it must seem to an imprisoned feline. It is now just over three weeks since she had the operation, and today Michael says to me that he feels that Titus's limp is getting worse and that she will never walk properly again, and that I should take her to our local vet to get her checked out with some speed, and this I do.

Pat, the local vet who had removed her stitches twelve days' post-operatively, is impressed with her recovery and doesn't think there is anything wrong at all, but reminds me how very serious the procedure has been and that there are internal wires and also, in spite of the restricted exercising, Titus will have lost a lot of muscle power in the period of her incarceration, so her limping is bound to be severe. In other words, we are just being neurotic parents.

CHAPTER 11

Jo and Damian have now returned to England and are living only a few miles away from us in a relatively remote cottage that a friend of theirs has kindly lent to them, and I find myself becoming surprisingly broody on Jo's behalf. In the role of stepmother-out-of-law, one is not properly allowed the indulgence of claiming grandmother-hood, but nevertheless I find that I am instinctively drawn towards this tall, young, elegant woman who is being very brave, and very positive, but who is experiencing all the anxiety of a first-time pregnancy, combined with the difficulty of being in a foreign country and away from her own mother and father in far-off Sweden. I long to give her as much comfort as I can. Their baby is due in under a month's time and Jo is carrying him, for *him* they know it to be, high and proud. Damian and Jo are both extremely conscientious about healthy dieting and healthy living for Jo (though Damian is not so strict on himself) and I am hugely impressed with Jo's own resolve. We go on a couple of shopping sprees, which are huge fun for me, and we buy all manner of baby things. In the evening after one of these shopping trips, as Michael and I sit down to have a meal together, I find myself saying:

'Michael, when we finally find a house and have moved in and settled down, the cats will obviously have more freedom and be able to go outside. Do you think that Pushkin at that point might actually get his act together and mate with Fannie or Titus?'

'Uh, uh! What's brought this on, eh?'

'Oh just, you know, the girls are getting on a bit and it would be so lovely if they could have one litter each.'

'I thought you told me that Titus wasn't supposed to have any kittens, and she's certainly in no state right now to be getting pregnant.'

'No, that's true, but when I asked Rob if he would neuter her at the same time as sorting out her patella, he said it was too much to inflict on her in one go, which made sense, so I suppose that is the next blimmin' hurdle for the poor old thing. But Fannie, maybe?'

'Marilyn, I think we should concentrate our energies on buying and selling houses right now.'

'Yup, maybe you're right – oh well, just a thought.'

Within the confines of Moon Cottage there is much coming and going. We have put the house on the market with a local estate agent, and quite quickly a couple of appointments with would-be buyers ensue. I begin to worry, as people come to view the house, as to what sort of perverts they might think we are when they come into our bedroom and find Titus cooped up dejectedly in her cage. A rather defensive pitch becomes the norm as I try to explain exactly why she is in the cage, and that really she is there for her own good.

While this is happening around Moon Cottage, Michael and I have been internet surfing to find properties in the north of England, which should ideally be:

- Away from any lethal roads so that the cats may have their freedom at last.
- Surrounded by hills, or in an oasis of peace and quiet and with far-reaching views.
- With a pub within decent reach for Michael.
- Not *too* isolated – being able to pick up the paper in the morning being an issue.
- Most importantly of all for one of us, within an hour's drive of Ewood Park, which is, I am led to understand, a piece of hallowed ground in the environs of Blackburn.
- Close to where Michael's mother is and close to several of his siblings.
- Close to Wensleydale where Geoffrey lives.
- The house itself must be an old building, preferably a farmhouse or cottage.

It all proves more difficult than one might think within our budget. Our chosen counties are North Yorkshire,

Cumbria and Lancashire. Each of us spends hours fantasy-shopping in this way; it truly is the stuff that dreams are made of.

Meanwhile, Johnny too is busy looking around nearer to home for a place of his own. Michael and I have both felt hugely guilty that our proposed move means that he now needs to find himself his own home, but Johnny, with his characteristic generosity of spirit, replies:

'No honestly, I needed a kick up the arse. If you hadn't both decided to do this, I would have been living with you till I was middle-aged.'

'Johnny, you are very welcome to live with us in the north of England; it would be wonderful if you would come,' I protest, and Michael of course endorses this fulsomely.

'No, sorry. Can't do *North*, just can't!' he retorts, omitting all explanation, although he is in a good job where he is in the south-east of England, which is reason enough, but I remain unsure if that is the sole basis for his reluctance. One night, soon after this, Johnny comes home very excited. He has found himself a property that he loves, and although it is more than he was budgeting for he is sure that it will be a good investment. The three of us go off to see it together that weekend and it is sweet. It is a tiny cottage down a quiet mews with one huge room downstairs and a kitchen and a utility room, and one bedroom and bathroom on the next floor, and a further bedroom on the top floor – it is like a teeny version of Moon Cottage in some ways, and it has an adorable walled courtyard behind, which is completely splendid for container plants. Michael and I are really happy for him. He will be able to exchange and complete in a couple of months, so we joke with him that he will be gone long before there is any movement on our front. But then, to my delight, Michael suddenly says:

'Look, I think we should start to physically recce now, because until we really start actually looking we are fumbling in the dark.'

'I agree, oh I agree, but what if we find somewhere really quickly?'

'Let's cross that bridge when we come to it.'

So we start our search in earnest and we distil down

to eight properties, but sadly they are spread all over the place between the Yorkshire Dales, Cumbria and Lancashire.

Michael does an advance recce of three further properties during a business visit to the North, and one of them in particular, a farmhouse near a lake in a secluded valley in Upper Wensleydale, I have high hopes for. Sadly, however, he gives it the thumbs down, and before I can see it for myself it has gone 'under offer'; but it needs us both to be on board, so I am content enough that it doesn't pass muster and we must 'move on'.

Our allotted weekend for the big excursion arrives and it is possibly the wildest and certainly the wettest weather forecast for the north of England that I have heard for a very long time. Michael remains undaunted and off we go. Our very first property, where we are to meet the agent, Richard, is just outside a remote village in Swaledale. The rain is completely horizontal and the wind must certainly be close to gale force, if not actually at it, and as we drive up the dale from the eastern side of the country, we have to negotiate our way round one fallen tree after another. We eventually discover the tiny single-track zigzag road that will lead us up to the farmhouse. As we start to ascend, we meet a large white van coming down, and although the accepted rule is other, the driver makes us reverse for him.

'I can't believe we're meeting white vans here, I thought we'd left all that behind in the commuter-lands of the South, and he's driving like a white-van-driver too,' Michael grunts crossly.

We continue our journey upwards and then, to Michael's incredulity, one of the several hairpin bends is so acute in its angle that it is necessary to reverse and go forward twice to get round it. We climb some more and finally arrive on the top of the hill where we find the building we have been looking for. It is a butty stone farmhouse, squat and low and very solid, and will clearly withstand many gales yet to come. It has a conservatory clamped on to the front of it, which is square and ugly and looks just like a reinforced glass box, and inside there is a row of six empty chairs all next to each other, for their potential occupiers to sit staring straight through the glass front at the view. The view today consists of solid cloud, which is enveloping the hillside in a blanket of thick dank fog, and the only visible movement is the driving rain mixing with the swirling cloud and some forlorn clumps of straggling brown grasses blowing wildly in the wind, and nothing else – not even a single sheep.

'This reminds me of an old-people's home, but less cheerful,' Michael observes, staring at the chairs in their regimented line. I try not to let him hear my despairing giggle.

'Michael, I know this part of Swaledale really well, and the view out there is breathtaking honestly. It's just the weather today.'

Richard hears my plea and does a sterling job as we walk round the rest of the building, finding a selling point here and another there, but it is quite clear that Michael cannot wait to get out, so there is little point in delaying our departure. Our descent is considerably easier, although there is no escaping the tortuous back and forth manoeuvre on the worst hairpin.

Thrown by our first joint foray I am now fearful of what lies ahead. We then see four different houses, all of which have several charms, but none of them has enough of our required ingredients, although we do see a house from the outside in a village called Thornton Rust in Wensleydale, which is close to where I used to live with Geoffrey. This house is charming, albeit on the small side, and it gives us hope. The saddest house of all, though, is in a village too far east to be practical for us, close to Richmond. The house is a large elegant Georgian farmhouse and looks tremendously attractive, but as we get close to it, to our horror we discover its frontage is on one of the busiest dual carriageways in Britain, the A66. People die regularly on that stretch of road, never mind cats.

Dales friends of ours, Thomas and Doreen, tell us about a farmhouse near the renowned Ribblehead Viaduct that has suddenly come on the market in the last twenty-four hours, and so with that and the Thornton Rust property in mind we talk to an agent in Hawes. I am having trouble concealing my excitement as I long to be back in this part of the world, and I so want one or other of these to be the one for us. We drive out to the Ribblehead farmhouse on the Sunday evening, just as it is getting dark, and again the wind is up. It is wild and very empty around there, but the views are magnificent and the skyscapes spectacular. We park the car and we both climb stiffly out, but the jacket Michael is wearing is only lightweight. As the wind tears at the back of it, he hauls it more firmly round his body and I can hear his teeth chattering; I too am pretty chilly, it must be admitted. I look at the expression on Michael's face. It is all screwed up against the wind and his teeth are clenched, but I detect an additional firmness in his jaw line that does not augur well.

'Getting a paper in the morning could be a bit of a problem.'

'Yes, but look, there's a pub only fifty yards away.'

'But what if we got snowed in and couldn't use the car, we would be completely trapped, and anyway it's too small.'

I know in my heart of hearts that this property isn't going to work and that he is right; it is blissfully secluded but also, paradoxically, the road could be a problem for the cats because remote though it is, it is the main road into Hawes from Settle and Ingleton, which produces its own weight of local traffic, added to which there is a great deal of tourist traffic for two-thirds of the year, and also bikers in their hundreds use that road. I know for a fact that the farmers who draw on the grazing that surrounds us, which is split into two by this largely unfenced road, are in despair at the number of lambs – and even sheep – they lose in collisions with cars every year.

My persistent concern about the cats being run over is both reinforced and dissipated by Richard telling me, when I raise it with him yet again, that when he and his wife lived in a village called Bampton, they were three miles down a track which had no traffic on it at all, and to their horror an oil delivery lorry filling up their tank for their central heating ran their cat over. They put food out that night as usual, and when the cat didn't come back they went looking, and found its squashed body the following day. They assumed that the driver didn't even know he had done it. So where on earth is actually safe? Inside a house I suppose.

The following day, Monday, we are due to see just two more properties, both in Cumbria, and then drive back south to Moon Cottage. We set off early in the morning and the first property we are to see is one that I initially found on the internet, but which then disappeared, and then I found it again being handled by a different estate agent. Technically, therefore, it is one of our properties, but Richard, whom I supplied with a list of our favourites, has offered to see it on our behalf in advance and has reported back to us that he thinks we should see it, but he is concerned that it might be too small. We say our farewell to Geoffrey and to Hawes and drive out past Ribblehead and out on to the main Kendal to Skipton road at Ingleton and turn up towards the little market town of Kirkby Lonsdale.

'Marilyn, the traffic on this road is awful.'

'I know, I avoid going on this road whenever possible, and it seems to be bad at all times of year too. The trouble is that the trans-Pennine routes are in short supply and this one goes south-east towards the industrial cities of West Yorkshire and cuts off a whole corner, so it's a really useful link road.'

'Humph, well I'm not impressed, is all I can say.' Soon, however, the signs for Kirkby Lonsdale are visible and we know we have to start looking for a side road to the left, which will lead us to the village where we have our first appointment. I have studied the map and can see a more direct road than the first turning and, mindful that first impressions are all important, I reckon we should go for the second turning. As we make the turn into my chosen route, to my amazement we find that the road is single track, but neither of us says anything. We drive slowly round a right-hand bend and go up a hill, past a little copse on the left, and suddenly there is grass growing out of the tarmac. Neither of us says a word and the grass continues its triumphant march down the middle of the road. After we swing round the fourth completely blind corner along this narrow road bordered by a mixture of dry stone walling and high hedges, Michael asks quietly:

'Was this the only way into the village?'

'No, but it looked like the most direct way on the map. We're nearly there now, honestly.'

'Good, glad to hear it – but it is very beautiful round here, look at those views.' We arrive at the end of this long, winding little road and turn right as we get to the main village street, passing the post office on the left, and start to climb up a steep hill. As we near the top, on the left we pass a grand-looking Victorian house standing back in its large garden, which we can see only in tiny snapshots through small gaps in the hedge. As we pass the end of the sweeping curved driveway into this large house we see an enormous ancient copper beech, with a breathtaking spread of branches growing from it, standing in the very centre of the driveway. This is the Old Vicarage and next to it is a very strange-looking building which is, it turns out, the Coach House – and our destination. In the details we have acquired from the estate agents, we know that this building was the original coach house to the vicarage, for whomsoever was the current incumbent of the church that stands higher up the road. Michael says:

'Let's just drive on a bit further and get a feel for the place.' We drive on up to the little church and stop the car there. The church is a charming Victorian sandstone building with a turreted square tower, surrounded by ancient yews and equally ancient-looking headstones and it announces itself boldly as St John's. We turn our backs to the church and gaze out across the valley to the distant hills. I squeeze Michael's arm:

'I think those are the Howgills, not sure, but could be – and look, that nearer one is probably Whernside! The brochure said you could see two of the Three Peaks from the house, and also Barbondale.'

Michael laughs with pleasure and squeezes my hand back.

'It certainly has a most "agreeable aspect", I must say, Mo, but wait until we have seen more.'

We get back into the car and drive back towards the Coach House. The most imposing thing when looking at the house is in fact the group of massive Scots pines (probably about ninety feet high), which are gathered together at one end of the garden. The house is high up and behind a thick evergreen hedge, so it is quite hard to see it fully from the road. We walk in and introduce ourselves to the owner, Pamela. Richard is yet to arrive. She shows us round the house with enthusiasm and clearly loves it herself. As we walk around it I become slightly mystified by it. It has two staircases to two separate bits of an upper floor, which are not connected to each other. We discover that this is because it has grown with each successive owner, who has added a bit on as they were able to afford it, so it has become an organic building; but there was never enough land to build another room at ground level to make it work like a normal house, room on room.

As we walk into what Pamela calls the guest suite at the southern end of the building, she walks us through a large bedroom with windows in three of the four walls, facing north, east and west, which makes it very light and airy, and then we are led into the large guest bathroom. This has a pair of floor-to-ceiling French windows with a balcony outside and one long high window down the other side too, so it is lit from the east and the west. As Pamela pulls aside the curtains and opens the French windows, she invites us to step on to the balcony. She laughs as she does this, admitting that all her life she had wanted a Juliet balcony and has had to wait until her middle years before she finally achieved it. At this point, Richard arrives and she goes down to greet him, leaving Michael and me alone. Michael is staring transfixed through the French windows at the view across the valley below and up to the high hills beyond.

'Well?' he demands urgently in a low voice. 'Well?'

'Yes, it's lovely, but do you . . . ?'

'Surely, this is it?'

'Just like that?'

'Don't you agree?'

'Yes, I do agree, but I'm just surprised that you have committed so quickly in this way.'

'But this is how it was with Moon Cottage, don't you remember? It was exactly the same.'

In fact, Moon Cottage surprised me because Michael fell in love as he walked through the front door, but it took me slightly longer. I didn't love it *completely* body and soul until I was in the dining room. But I am thrilled that he feels this way about the Coach House and I find I share his feelings. Interestingly, when the moment comes, all the things on the 'must have' list of requirements become suddenly less mandatory if the house is right, so neither he nor I discuss any of those at this stage. One thing, however, that has pleased me hugely during the time we have been here is the absence of traffic. We have seen one lorry and one tractor go past in something like an hour. The garden is small and interesting and there is a way round the back, over a fence, into an enormous field and beyond that is a woodland, and hanging above that, we learn, is an outstanding limestone pavement known as Hutton Roof Crags, so there are endless possibilities of explorations for the cats.

As Richard walks into the room on his own, Michael tells him quietly that we are about to cancel the next viewing appointment, and Richard beams happily at the prospect of a done deal. We go downstairs and ask Pamela as many questions as we can think of in connection with the house and the garden. There is a room downstairs, which Michael has already nominated as his study cum library, but which is currently set up as

Pamela's studio where, we discover, she works on her sculptures. There are several hand-carved boxwood miniature animals and birds on one of the tables, and when I ask her about them I discover that she is about to exhibit in London at the invitation of the Royal Society of Miniature Painters, Sculptors and Gravers, for which she subsequently receives one of the Society's most prestigious awards and is presented to HRH the Prince of Wales. Her sculptures (technically okimonos rather than netsukes, because they are miniatures in their own right, rather than toggles for kimonos) are truly beautiful and it is motivating to contemplate living in a house that has been inhabited by someone who cares about the natural world and has such obvious artistic talent. Pamela is also a skilled nurseryman and has grown a range of extremely interesting perennials for sale for some years, which has hugely benefited the garden.

As we somewhat breathlessly take our leave and cross the road to the car, Pamela suddenly calls out over the hedge:

'If you do want it you'd better hurry up, there's

another couple coming this afternoon, they have just been on the phone now.'

'Don't worry, we're off now to start things rolling,' Michael calls back.

CHAPTER 12

When we are alone and finally able to talk freely to each other, Michael and I find we have no doubts at all that the village of Hutton Roof and the Coach House within it are where we would love to spend the rest of our days. On our return to Moon Cottage, therefore, there is much to be done. We have to set in motion the raising of money to buy the Coach House. One young couple who have already seen Moon Cottage once are clearly interested in it, but openly admit that the price is out of their bracket; our hopes are high, though, as they have asked us if they might send round an independent valuer, which we interpret as good news.

Meanwhile, we know from both Richard and also from Pamela herself that there is not much time to play with, as Pamela has already bought a property in France and has a moving date organised – and is therefore compelled to sell to the first buyer she gets. The French system for buying and selling houses is similar to the Scottish one, which means that once you have committed, that is it, and the date for exchange of monies is set in stone. We are terrified that our newly discovered earthly paradise will slip through our fingers and so, without more ado, Michael goes into action and, with the aid of a helpful broker, we manage to raise a second mortgage, commission a solicitor recommended to us by our agent and make our offer for the purchase of the Coach House. The sale is agreed and the ball starts to roll.

Back at the cottage I am beginning to let Titus out of her cage for longer and longer periods, but am increasingly frightened of her jumping up or down. On three occasions now she has jumped down from the bed before I could stop her in spite of the 'Lady of Shalott' mirror arrangement; and I have been severely warned about the dangers of her undoing her surgery, which would be dire. Her spirits are so low, though, and she clearly doesn't understand why she is incarcerated in this way; I really fear what her interpretation must be of the treatment she is receiving at my hands. Six weeks' imprisonment is a long time. In part to try to compensate for this 'cruelty', I spend long periods of time with her on my knee, or, as a variation, with her lying on my desk, where I will stroke her and talk to her, to try to make her feel loved. I have also noticed that she and Fannie seem to be almost closer now than ever before, even taking into account that they have always been devoted from early kittenhood (Fannie's nastiness to Titus post-operatively excepted), but the fact that they can't sleep together seems to have reinforced their bond rather than severed it, by providing them with a form of yearning for each other. As an experiment, for the sake of Titus's morale, I tried putting Fannie in the cage with her, but had to abandon it due to the fuss (from Fannie, of course, not Titus, who was clearly up for it).

And now, at last, the day has come when I can take

Titus back to our local vet, Pat, to get clearance to allow her the liberty she craves. I am a little concerned in case some of the jumps have caused irreversible damage, but Pat gives her the all clear and feels that her recovery is on the right track, and that we just need to be very careful with her, especially when we let her outside. I am more concerned, knowing the cottage, about the stairs as they are so very steep. When we get home and finally fold away her cage, she seems truly unbelieving and, in fact, as we start to go to bed she is unsure herself where to sleep, so I lay down the big duvet cushion that has been her bed morning, noon and night since the operation, exactly where the cage has been, and she does indeed sleep on that, although after about half an hour I hear her jumping up on to the low armchair that she and Fannie consider their own piece of furniture. Indeed, the following day, for the sake of her peace of mind, I reinstate the cage with the door open for a couple more nights until she is properly ready to re-enter the 'real' world. Later on, in that first night of freedom, I hear her slowly clump her way downstairs to the litter tray in the kitchen, and it wrenches my heart to hear her hobbling down, sounding like Blind Pew. Pat had said to me, however, that she needs to build up those muscle tissues, and this form of exercise is what is required to strengthen them, so I let her be. So, for the first time in six weeks, Michael and I enjoy a night's sleep without the accompaniment of the sound and smells of a bored and pissed-off cat on auto-pilot apparently, burying, interminably, something the size of a haunch of venison in a tray of cat litter.

Since the ominous warning in late January from my sister, Judy, in America, things have gone from bad to worse and she is currently intensively nursing Rod at home, but it is clear that his cancer is terminal, and nothing can be done to save him. The courage of that family is considerable though. Rod remains cheerful and sparkly, and from time to time I talk to him on the phone and am astonished at his strength of character, although it shouldn't surprise me. He was always doughty and the same applies to his three children, Mark, Claire and Emma, the last of whom is herself expecting a baby, which is especially tough at this time; but it is Judy, in a different way, to whom I doff my cap. There is nothing that she will not do for her man, however gruesome or arduous, and it is this that makes it possible for him to remain at home and experience as full and as rewarding a quality of life as the circumstances will allow him. She too is full of optimism and shows the most amazing fortitude. I admire them all more than I can say.

Here on this side of the Atlantic, the baby-making is going apace. Jo and I meet up for a girlie lunch on Friday, and by this time she is ten days' overdue and has been told by her midwife at the hospital that if she does not go into labour naturally over the weekend, they will induce labour on the Monday – which she is desperate to avoid, wanting the birth to be as natural as possible. She is now beginning to feel very uncomfortable and very tense, and who wouldn't be? As we are driving down the road just chatting about this and that, she says to me in a low voice, so low I can hardly hear her:

'Marilyn, I think you should know that I am having contractions closer together now.' I squawk back in a very uncool sort of way:

'Jo, how long have you been having these contractions?'

'Oh, a little while.'

'Jo, I think we should go to the hospital, what do you say?'

'Do you really think so?'

'Yessssssssssssss.'

So we go to the hospital where she is booked in to give birth, and the problem with being a mother-out-of-law is that it gets difficult to throw your weight around, so I become a mother-in-law for convenience's sake. And the upshot is that she is contracting, but the baby is way off and she is only in the first stage, so, at her firm request, I take her back home and wait with her until Damian, who has been playing golf all day, finally gets home and fusses around her and is clearly set to take the best possible care of her when I take my leave of them while they brace themselves for the very last stage of their old life together before the staggering first stage of their brand-new life, when they will be three, stretching out ahead of them.

Her contractions continue in a mild way for the remainder of Friday, but on Saturday morning she wakes up at 4 a.m. and they are coming five minutes apart. By 5 a.m. she is strapped into a borrowed Land Rover and Damian starts the drive into Watford to the hospital. As they are en route her waters break, but they keep going (although I suspect that Damian is busy having proverbial kittens by this time) and arrive safely at the hospital and then, brave girl that she is, Jo delivers her baby in a stoically squatting position, taking a chunk out of Damian's shoulder in her last push to expel him (the baby that is, not Damian, she assures me!), and at 9.10 a.m. on the Saturday morning a little boy is born, called Oskar William Herbert, weighing in at 9 lbs 6 oz. I will never, for as long as I live, forget the expression of pleasure on Michael's face when he first holds Oskar. I have to say the expression of pride on Damian's face was pretty cool too!

Four days later, Emma in America gives birth to her

son, Alex, who has decided to enter the world a staggering four weeks early, unlike the laidback Oskar, and he weighs in at 6 lbs and 9 oz. With considerably more difficulty than Jo, Emma too finally gets to introduce her son to his paternal grandfather.

Suddenly, on the house-buying front, there is an unexpected complication. Our solicitor's conveyancing clerk (the solicitor himself is on holiday for almost the full period of the conveyancing, as is Richard, our buying agent, so we totally lack advisers) tells us that if we are to exchange and complete by the end of April, which is the date required by Pamela to meet her French move, we will all have to vacate Moon Cottage, because our mortgage agreement is on a buy-to-let basis and these are the rules, but not only that, we must also be resident at the new house in Hutton Roof at the point of exchange; and if we are not in residence (we had intended to be on holiday in France) he tells us, it will constitute mortgage fraud.

It had not originally been our intention to move to Hutton Roof immediately, as Michael is still in full-time work, but rather we planned to move once he leaves at the end of May. This decree demoralises us beyond words because it will be impossible for us to move our furniture in the time left, so we will move up to Hutton Roof without furniture, with cats who will hate it, without anything, not even a bed, and Michael will be commuting to London without a home, and will have to find accommodation elsewhere.

Oliver and his girlfriend Lisa come up from Wales to stay with us as we all wake up to the fact that life is about to change in a radical way, and the next time we see Ollie we will be living in the North and everything will be different. Oliver is working towards his finals, and also he has now taken the major decision to sell up the business that was his mother's and that he has been running since her sudden death last autumn; and once that is sorted, he has decided that he would love to travel the world.

As soon as Oliver and Lisa have returned to Wales I set about trying to find removal companies with the earliest possible date for our furniture to be taken up and, having phoned five companies, the best I can achieve is three weeks away but, to satisfy our conveyancing clerk, what is important is that we three residents are physically no longer domiciled in Moon Cottage and that, of course, must include the cats.

The French trip was to have involved a week's holiday for Michael and me, together with his brother John, visiting our friends Geoff and Pat in their house in Poitiers. The return flight has been booked for months and as soon as the conveyancing clerk tells us to pull the plug on it we try to get a refund from the airline, but of course that proves impossible. Cancelling our trip like this also means that Geoff and Pat, who could have rented out our accommodation to someone else, have lost that opportunity too. John, because he is an incredibly kind and generous-spirited person, offers to come up to Hutton Roof instead with us, as he had booked the holiday anyway, to help us do whatever needs to be done there.

This last week before we leave for Hutton Roof the action around the cottage is pretty intense, in every possible way, and I become very aware that the cats are anxious, even alarmed, as everything is other than it normally would be, so now, of course, I feel guilty as I have not been able to think about them, or properly spend time with them in the way that I should.

In spite of the chaos reigning within Moon Cottage I manage to secure the longed-for post-operative appointment with Titus's surgeon, Rob, who intently watches her walking. He is pleased with the results of the operation on her right leg and feels that it should hold for her lifetime, but I am fearful that he will say that the time has come to look at her left leg again. Before allowing him to speak, I fulsomely express my reservations about the cruelty to my mind of the necessarily severe confinement a further operation on Titus would entail and how, unless it is a matter of life and death, I really don't want to do this to Titus; it would utterly mess with her quality of life, and so what does he think? I know as I make my lengthy and impassioned statement that I am probably forcing him into a difficult situation, and he pauses a long time before he does reply. The essence of his reply is that the correction to her right leg may be enough to keep her left leg in place, but I am going to need to watch it like a hawk, because if it does spontaneously pop out again, as it did under manipula-

tion, then it will need addressing, but for the moment
Titus can go free. I want to hug him, but due to his
extreme youth I control myself, and skip out of his
consulting room with Titus jiggling around in the cat
cage, eyes large and mildly concerned.

CHAPTER 13

Our enforced moving day encroaches upon us and for several days now the cats have been noticeably tense. Titus is on heat and now Fannie has joined her, and they are both squawking raucously, but Pushkin is the one who is surprising me. He has a rather disarming, quite girly alto squeak, and for two days he has been talking away all over the house, to me and to himself, at repeated intervals; as he is normally a quiet cat, it is significant. This morning, from first thing, he goes into hiding and although I know I am going to have to find him ultimately, for the moment at least it seems better just to leave him. Michael goes early to the office in

London to do most of a day's work, but around mid-afternoon – it being a Friday – he will drive straight up to Cumbria from London in his own car and collect his brother, John, from the local station of Oxenholme. Michael's son Johnny, meanwhile, packs his suitcase and departs for his office in his car, and at the end of his working day he will then drive down to the West Country to stay with friends, and on his return his plan is to stay in Watford with another friend.

After they have both left, the house is suddenly very quiet and I feel sick because we have somehow been bullied out of Moon Cottage and this is not the way I had wanted to move into our new home. Slowly I start to pack up my own car for the long trek north, with the cats being the last addition. They are all prone to carsickness, but Fannie and Pushkin especially, and I have not yet found any medication that a vet will sanction for feline travel-sickness; it exists for dogs, but sadly not for cats. With my three on longer excursions – I cage them on short journeys, for ease and safety – I find that if they are left free in the back of the car (with a grill separating them from the driver) they travel better. This also means I can leave out a cat litter tray and a bowl of water, and all three of them make use of both. I think the freedom of movement allows the balance in their inner ear to adjust itself more easily. On long car journeys, Fannie watches out of the window, certainly in daylight hours, and I am sure that helps her. Pushkin tends to bury himself low down in the car under blankets and newspapers and that almost certainly *doesn't* help him. Titus is the least problematical traveller and usually sits quite still, letting it all happen.

The house at Hutton Roof has no furniture in it at all, so I cram the car with as many artefacts to keep us going as I can think of, including the all-important self-inflating mattresses. It is now raining hard and I discover I have left no room for the cat-carrying cage. I start to look for the cats and I find Pushkin head down under a pile of clothes in our wardrobe, not a very good hiding place, as it was bound to be where I would look first, but that's Pushkin for you, so I grab him in my arms and manage to push him through a tiny opening in the car door and shut it again. I repeat the same exercise with Titus, but Fannie proves to be more difficult. A few days earlier I had fallen down the steps of the estate agent's office and I am still recovering from a severely sprained left ankle and swollen right shoulder, and I simply cannot manhandle her into the car on my own, as my immobile shoulder is becoming a major hindrance; so I take her back into the cottage, but I'm close to tears of frustration. Stephen from next door suddenly appears and nobly helps me, so between us we manage to force the unwilling Fannie into the car, narrowly avoiding her wriggling free to run out into the now heavy traffic; but just as we get the car door closed, a small van shoots past us through a massive puddle, comprehensively soaking us both. The three cats inside the car start up a miaowing and a mewling, and at that point my mobile goes and it is Pamela from Hutton Roof, sounding worried and impatient, because she hasn't had the confirmation from her solicitor that the exchange and completion has gone through. I know that it has because I have had the confirmation from our conveyancing clerk, but I eventually discover that the reason Pamela doesn't know this is because her phone has been disconnected pending its reconnection in our name; but as I listen to her agitation, my own stress levels rise up into the red zone.

As I set off, the rain gets heavier and my mobile goes again; it is Michael, who suddenly wants us to reconsider whether we should accept a revised offer from the couple on Moon Cottage. Distraught with all that lies ahead of me, I just keep repeating that I don't know, I don't know, but I thought we, that is to say he, I and the agent had all agreed that the offer was way too low. He vacillates a little, and then he disconsolately agrees that is right and rings off. In truth, I don't pay much attention to this call, as I don't believe he is serious and there is so much else on my mind.

The journey is long and tedious, but for the main part – the motorway part of it – the cats, although unhappy, are not ill. But then close to Lancaster, because of a flagged-up accident higher up the motorway and warnings of queues and stationary traffic, we leave the motorway two junctions earlier than I had intended and do a tortuous cross-country route, at which point we get the full feline monty in the form of vomiting and diarrhoea from all three of them, preceded and followed by the most plaintive mewling. I daren't stop because I am scared of opening the back doors and letting them out, and I cannot access them through the grill from the front, so in spite of the severe assault on two of our five senses I keep going, singing songs very loudly to take all our minds off everything.

The delays at the beginning and then the travail of the journey itself now means that Michael is further ahead of schedule than I am, and by the time I roll up to the village of Hutton Roof he and John have already found the hidden key, unlocked the door and opened up. I stop and wearily get out and open up the stinking car. With John and Michael's help, the three of us manage to shepherd the cats into the empty house. Fannie and Titus hang around near us, clearly frightened. Although there are carpets in most of the rooms, without furniture the house is very echoey and noisy and there are almost no high surfaces for the cats to climb up on to. The second we get the cats inside, however, Pushkin just takes off and none of us sees where he goes.

'It's fine, Mo, there are no open windows, there is

nowhere he can go other than
inside the house, so he'll
be fine. Let's get that
car unpacked. Come on,
we'll come and help
you.' And so the
three of us begin the
wearisome task of
transferring the
goods and chattels
from the car into the house.
Each of the stairways consists
of uncarpeted, highly varnished
honey-coloured Paraná pinewood, and it is our intention
to leave them exactly as they are. But every time any
one of us goes up or down the stairs, either flight, the
clumping noise is deafening and it is visibly worrying
the two female cats; Pushkin, of course, is nowhere to
be seen. I sort out fresh cat litter for the tray, and then
put out some dried food and water. I know that soon I
must go and find Pushkin.

Michael has had the foresight to bring up and unpack

a couple of bottles of wine and even a corkscrew, and so we pull up the chairs around the little card table, open the wine with a flourish, and make a solemn toast to the house, and then, visibly relaxing, we each contentedly slurp away at the contents of our glass. The day has consisted of a series of heavy rainstorms for the greater part of the journey, and since our arrival up here it has been overcast. Now it is officially past sunset, but at the very last minute, before the sun finally sinks behind the limestone crag above the western side of the house, it makes a brave, last-ditch attempt at a watery welcome, and suddenly, as we are looking out through the east-facing windows of the conservatory, the dying rays of the sun from behind us throw out a blood-red reflection across the clouds, across the sky, and across the hills of Yorkshire. Everything as far as the eye can see is ablaze in its glow, and most spectacular of all is the highlighting of the great peak of Ingleborough, which is exactly due east of where we are by about twelve miles as the crow flies; and as we watch, every nook and cranny etched into that ancient hillside is clearly discernible and then, just as suddenly, the sun behind us drops below the horizon, the light changes, it darkens, and the moment has gone.

Sighing happily, Michael leans forward and touches my knee.

'Come on, Mo, time to go and find the boy.'

'OK. I'll go to the south bit and you look in the north bit.'

John goes off with Michael and I rootle around in what will be Michael's study and our bedroom, but I cannot find Pushkin anywhere. I can hear them calling him from the other side of the house, but as long as their voices can still be heard, they clearly haven't found him. Eventually I go back to join them, and John says:

'I think, I just think, that I might know where he is.'

'Where, for goodness sake?'

'I don't know how he got in there, but behind the sink.'

And, sure enough, Pushkin has found a hole that looks far smaller than would accommodate him, through which he has wiggled and, having crawled in there, he has followed the pipes right along the kitchen wall under the sink, behind the newly fitted kitchen units that were Pamela's pride and joy. For all we know, as we cannot see him properly, he could be stuck. The best we have managed so far is to shine a torch down at an oblique angle and we can just see his eyes glowing back.

'You are assuming it's Pushkin. It might not be,' I offer, possibly less than helpfully.

'Blimey, Marilyn, if it's not Pushkin, it's the biggest rat in creation!'

'The only solution is to pull out the fridge,' John, the peacemaker, suggests more helpfully. And so, with much effort and rather destroying the whole ethos of a fitted unit, the three of us haul out the fridge and, with the aid of a long broom handle, poke and pull and eventually grab, partly by his tail I am ashamed to say, the cat Pushkin. He emerges, terrified, covered from head to tail in cobwebs as if he had just surfaced from Miss Havisham's fossilised wedding feast.

'Block that hole up now,' Michael shouts assertively and we jump to it. (Rather sadly, we have never been able to reinstate the fridge as it should be, and the unit now is definitely a couple of inches proud of being fitted, and rocky to boot.)

I nurse Pushkin and gently try to coerce him to eat a little, which eventually he does, but he looks over his shoulder the whole time and crouches low and defensively on the ground. I then place him in the cat litter tray just in case after we have gone to bed he is too scared to try, and by dint of blocking his exit out of it (it is a covered one), after a few minutes I hear him make use of it. I then release him and off he runs.

'Let him go, he has to find somewhere he will be comfortable.'

After one more glass of wine and having, noisily, blown up the air beds with their built-in electronic pumps, which sound as if we are vacuuming a wooden floor with the loudest Hoover in the world, and which sets the cats off running for cover, we retire to our separate wings for our first night's sleep in Hutton Roof.

CHAPTER 14

I have brought up with me the big squashy duvet bed that Titus used while she was recovering from her operation, which I am fairly confident that the two girls will share, and I also brought a little circular cat bed that Pushkin sometimes sleeps on in Moon Cottage. During the night I am woken repeatedly by loud clunking noises which, it turns out, are the two girls walking up and down the stairs; cats can sound surprisingly heavy on wooden stairs I now realise. However, for most of the night Fannie and Titus sleep in the sitting room, but Pushkin's whereabouts remain a mystery. In the morning, as Michael starts the breakfast, of which in our household he is undisputed 'king', John and I go on a further Pushkin-hunt.

Eventually we find him jammed into the acute angle under the stairs behind a wall in Michael's study, on a tiny scrap of folded-up carpet. His chosen corner is very cobwebby, a bit damp and slightly musty smelling, which means that when I haul Pushkin out he too possesses these qualities. I hold him down by a bowl of cat food and he eats quickly, but he is clearly terrified, as he was yesterday. I then encourage him into the cat tray and again he uses it, but only under duress, and although I try to get him to lie on his bed, as soon as I take my hand off him he runs straight under the stairs again. In fact, he tries to get back to the pipes under the sink, but we have effectively blocked them off, so he is forced by default into the below-stairs position.

Because of our enforced move here the three of us are staying in the house with very little tackle between us. We have few changes of clothes and no tools of any kind, but as we rattle around the empty house we realise that as we are prisoners here, we might as well start doing useful things. We quickly discover that there is a big DIY store on the outskirts of Kendal and we take it in turns to do the run for various bits and pieces. I feel guilty while all this is going on, because I have to return the proofs of my book to my publisher and have a tight deadline, so while John and Michael work incredibly hard on the house, I try to shut myself away in one of the empty rooms to work on the proofs. That, in itself, is quite a challenge as we have so little furniture, and my table is an upended wooden crate.

Gerard, a younger brother to Michael and John, drives over to see us all, with his wife Sandra and sons Ryan and Benjamin. They very kindly bring over with them a large stripper-steamer which John and Michael are itching to get their hands on so they can start to strip off the various layers of wallpaper that festoon every room. On the very first morning I managed to break the shower fitment which controls the temperature of the water in our bathroom, and ever since then water has been pouring out of the wall – so poor Gerard finds that he is also required to mend that, and, being the excellent plumbing engineer that he is, he does –

but I fear he is going to be wary of any further invitations to the Coach House!

Michael and John set to work with the stripper and the noise and the steam and the mess is indescribable, and it goes on for days. Needless to say, the sound of the stripper truly petrifies the cats, but I feel I cannot ask the boys to stop because it makes them feel better that they are actually doing something useful, and anyway it desperately needs doing. Whichever room I take myself off to, I find that Titus and Fannie come and join me, but I am completely unable to persuade Pushkin to leave his bolt hole under the stairs; it is, however, one of the few places where the steamer won't be used. When he does come out, he does it crawling on his belly.

The one thing that makes him change his behaviour, just slightly, is if Titus or Fannie, but especially Titus, is near him. Then his actions alter, subtly, but discernibly. His body movements start as those of a cat crawling on his belly in fear, but as he sees Titus he raises himself fractionally and instead assumes the air of one stalking low and slinking along. He wants to crawl, his instinct is making him crawl, but he doesn't want to lose his standing in her eyes. I am enchanted to discover this particular strain of feline prevarication, although I am unhappy for his distress. I hide my smile from him.

On our second night in Hutton Roof we receive a kind-hearted invitation to have drinks with Annabel and Richard who live in the 'big' house next door, The Old Vicarage, of which our house was its original Coach House, so effectively we live in their garage!

I am mildly disconcerted when I answer the door to Richard, who is issuing the invitation, by his helpful codicil of 'don't dress up', knowing that we only have the clothes we are standing up in at that moment or, at best, an identical alternative. And seconds later, I am even more disconcerted when he spies Fannie trotting across the hallway and adds:

'Oh what a splendid pair of gloves that one would make!' She pauses and stares at him levelly, and trots off again waving her wild tail.

Their house is a typical small Victorian mansion with an attractive wooded garden full of flowering shrubs, plants and tall trees and, of course, the same breathtaking view as ours over the Barbon fells and the peaks of Yorkshire, including the great Ingleborough. Annabel and Richard are animated hosts and the wine and whisky flow freely and we talk of many things. One of the subjects that interests me greatly, however, is the problem of the wind farms, which are peppering Cumbria outside the national park, and there is a strong lobby afoot to build yet more. I had assumed until this evening that wind farms were an ecologically 'good thing'. As we talk more seriously about them, I begin properly to understand that the issue is truly compli-

cated, but that one of the major stumbling blocks is that onshore wind farming costs more than twice as

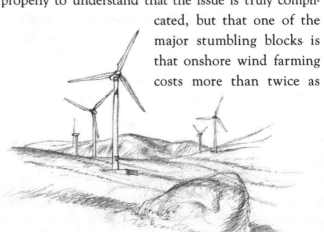

much per kilowatt-hour as most fossil fuels and also that payback time on the cost of construction takes six to seven years. They are clunky and ugly and noisy, they damage and interfere with wildlife, and while the landowner himself receives generous payment for playing host to a wind farm, his neighbours who suffer the horrors of it receive nothing at all. There is also the additional question of fair dispersal. Cumbria, this most beautiful of English counties, is already the site of much nuclear technology for the purposes of supplying and disposing of the resultant waste of Britain's energy, and many locals feel they have done more than enough in providing electricity for the rest of the UK. Although Cumbria is a county of high unemployment, more wind farms would not generate more employment in the county as they are operated remotely and maintained sparingly. Although I have very mixed feelings about nuclear power, I do begin, slowly, to see that this might be the better way forward until perhaps the scientists can crack the problem of energy from fusion. Additionally, money could be invested in offshore wind farming, which does not seem to arouse so many objections.

But wind farming is not all that we talk of and, only slightly comforted by Annabel's tinkling laughter, I rise to Richard's bait as he announces:

'You know about the rule that cats in this village are only allowed a maximum of 300 yards from their house for hunting?'

'Blimey, no, I don't! Whose rule is that?'

'My rule. I'm a serious songbird lover,' he replies crisply, with no outward show of merriment. I look across at Annabel for some sign of reassurance. She beams happily at me and shrugs. Richard then sets my mind at rest that really he is all right – well all right-ish at any rate – about cats as he tells me about a cat that adopted him in a tented camp in Nicosia when on National Service in 1956. The cat, a pure black moggy, slept in his tent and spent the day in and around the officers' mess tent. The cat was quickly adopted by the regiment as its mascot and named Maiwand after a regimental battle honour gained in Afghanistan in 1880. Maiwand, the cat, quickly learned to use cat initiative to lead a very feather-bedded existence in the camp, living off begged scraps, and every night, as soon as she heard the tinkle of coffee cups after dinner, she advanced down the mess miaowing plaintively to force the Colonel of the regiment, who traditionally always had first pull at the coffee tray, to pour her a saucer of milk. Richard describes how one evening he found her in the process of despatching a three-foot snake, which took more than half-an-hour with the cat jumping backwards and cuffing the snake each time it struck. Behaving, in fact, just like a mongoose. Eventually one cuff struck home and Maiwand had a particularly good dinner that night. This story of Maiwand leads Richard on, inexorably, to a story about a dog called Bobbie. I hold up my hands laughing, protesting enough, but he explains that in order to understand his cat Maiwand, I need to understand about Bobbie too. So here it is!

Bobbie, a small white mongrel with red ears and red eye patches, was a pet dog belonging to one Sergeant Kelly, but was also the pet of the entire Second Battalion of the Royal Berkshire Regiment (formerly the Sixty-sixth Regiment), which was severely beaten in the ill-fated battle of Maiwand in the Second Afghan War in 1880. There were many fatal casualties but the dog, although wounded, survived and then became lost on the battlefield during the retreat. He reappeared several days later to rejoin his regiment at Kandahar, over fifty miles away. In June 1881 Bobbie, along with many men and officers and one horse, was presented to Queen Victoria at the royal residence, Osborne House, where she placed the Afghan Medal around his neck. In spite of surviving all of this, just eighteen months later Bobbie suffered the ignominy of being run over and killed by a hansom cab in Gosport, at which point the regiment had the dog stuffed and put in a glass case. And I am now, courtesy of Richard, the proud possessor of a copy of that postcard in which Bobbie is, for all eternity, sporting his Afghan Medal.

Soon after that we meet several other neighbours, including Iain and his wife, Judy, who live at a farm a couple of miles away and who run a bed and breakfast. As well as helping Judy in the running of their guest-house business, Iain works as a carpenter and loves nothing better than challenging commissions in wood. Michael has asked him to measure up his study in order to line it, floor to ceiling, with unusually deep bookshelves so that he may double stack his myriad signed first editions, the collecting and exchanging of which is now going to become his full-time hobby. He is desperate for Iain to be able to complete the job before we actually move all the books up from Moon Cottage, so the pressure of time is on. We also need some gates for the driveway and, to Iain's much greater pleasure, a long narrow refectory table to fit into our long narrow conservatory, which will double up as our dining area.

When Iain arrives this morning for his final measuring-up trip I bemoan the chaos and mess that is being generated by the three of us gutting the house, which day by day is getting worse.

'Oh I know, it all looks terrible now, but think of the end result when the pain stops!' and I know he is right. I worry, however, when he adds that the long wet dark winters of Westmorland can be quite demoralising and the sixty inches of rainfall a year are pretty spectacular. I think, until that moment, Michael has not realised quite how high the incidence of rainfall in Cumbria actually is. It is, after all, the *lake* district.

We persuade Geoffrey to drive over to see the Coach

House from his home in Hawes, which, we have now measured, is twenty-five miles by road. I am on tenter-hooks prior to this meeting as it somehow matters inordinately that he approves of our choice. He arrives and takes one look out across the valley and up towards the hills whence he has just emerged and says quietly:

'Oh yes, oh yes. Look at that!' and I am utterly thrilled. Later on he says that he actually feels mildly jealous, as although he is in the heart of the Dales his view does not compare with ours, and my cup flows over!

Michael and John and I each spend hours just gawping out of the conservatory window at those breathtaking distant views of Ingleborough and the Howgills and the Barbon fells. The truth is that even in the rain they are magnificent, and when the cloud is down, they are still enchanting, as the mist gives an air of mystery to everything. Michael quickly develops a theory that when it rains 'the hills walk away' as they hide behind the cloud cover. But in this first week we are lucky, and although there is rain, there is also sun aplenty; watching the changing light scudding across the hills and the ever-changing colour is mesmerising. As I look out, I feel so happy that we are here now, but when I turn in and look at the house that we seem to be wrecking evermore, day by day, with a group of three very unhappy cats in attendance, then I wonder what on earth are we doing?

CHAPTER 15

Every day that we stay at the Coach House – actually I discover it is properly called *The Old* Coach House – it continues to be uncomfortable for the two queens, but it is tantamount to a nightmare for the poor little tom. Although I thought it was going to be bad for them all, in the event it is so much worse, for Pushkin in particular, that I am filled with remorse. Three times a day I go into the alcove under the stairs in Michael's study and haul out my protesting boy and take him first to the food and water bowls and then to the cat litter tray. He suffers all these indignities and then runs back to his hidey-hole. Fannie tries to find the height she craves but, with lack of furniture other than banisters and door tops, she is hard-pressed in her quest; she does, however, manage to climb the stepladder quite efficiently. Both she and Titus spring up and down off every windowsill continually, Titus more creakily, but they are a height she can just manage, and Fannie, to my complete horror, repeatedly walks the banister rail around the top of our stairwell – and I sense that she actually enjoys my fear. Otherwise, the two girls just clump the stairs.

While we are here I am able to access the internet from my computer, balanced on the upturned crate, and I email Margot about the plight of the cats. She replies to me, forwarding an old email she had from a close friend of hers in France, Jacqueline, who, when she wrote this email, had just moved house from Paris to Ouistreham, complete with her two neutered toms – magnificently named Brigadoon and Sir Mortimer. Her move created some pretty big issues for her boys too it would seem!

Dear Margot

Let me tell you how awful and terrifying it was here Sunday evening when Brigadoon and Sir Mortimer got into an all-out war, looking like a fight to the death. And I was in the middle, trembling, bombarding the warriors with pans of cold water, or trying that old Roman arena thing – you know, throwing the net, but using blankets and quilts instead. Finally, Sir M got out from under a blanket, Brigadoon pounced on it, and I was in the midst of dragging the blanket along, with Brigadoon on board, to the nearby closet when Sir M clawed at my left hand. Nonetheless, I continued pulling the blanket to the closet door, shoved Brigadoon in with my foot, closed the door, and then grabbed a dishtowel in the kitchen to wrap around my combat wounds dripping on the tile floor. Sir Mortimer wandered about a bit and then went out of the open backdoor to the garden. I immediately locked it, let Brigadoon out of the closet, and commenced putting compresses of disinfectant on my left hand and arm. At 1.30 a.m. I went to bed, and woke up an hour later. The two cats were again howling and grumbling and I could hear them banging into the glass door (storm windows luckily) that opens on to the garden. They were still trying to fight through the glass panes, terrifying . . .

Early the next morning I let Sir M into the garage under the house, gave him food, water, a blanket and a makeshift litterbox and shut and locked the adjoining door . . . Brigadoon was meanwhile shut inside in the rest of the house . . .

I then went to a nearby vet clinic that was recommended to me and told them what had happened. They didn't seem surprised and explained that it was caused by a territorial issue and stress because of moving, and with the help of two happy-pheromone distributors that plug into electrical sockets all should be well. It takes twenty-four hours for them to work. So I plugged them in, and by yesterday evening Brigadoon was purring or lying around tummy up, which means relaxed. Sir M was still in the garage while the house filled up with pheromones.

We are now living in this feline equivalent of an opium den, all doors and windows closed so we do not lose any of the precious divine atmosphere. The heart of the matter seems to be who owns the left corner of the living room couch, perceived as the prime piece of napping real estate by both parties. Today I moved the couch to a different wall. Now the boys are sprawled around the house napping here and there, not seeming to have a care in the world, no doubt meditating lazily on the changing geometry of couches.

Lots of love,
Tiger Mum Jacqueline

Margot sends this to me with the suggestion that I acquire some of this magical plug-in pheromone. I then email my friend Elspeth as I remember she said she had a terrible time with her two cats, the young neutered tom, Arthur, and his mother, Freya, when she moved earlier this year, and ask her to remind me exactly what happened:

From:	Elspeth
To:	Marilyn
Sent:	Thursday, 6 May, 11:17
Subject:	Arthur

```
Hi
   Basically, on the morning of the
move I put their food down to get
them in the open and then grabbed
Arthur, tried to get him in the cage
you lent me and, as you warned, the
door fell off and he just jumped out
and ran into the bedroom and hid under
the bed.
   I got Freya in the other cage, and
then went into the bedroom and shut
the door. I took the mattress off the
bed, and could see him under the slats
```

of the bed, at which point he started howling. I leant the bed frame against the wall, and the only place left for him to hide (which was rubbish, but he is quite thick) was behind the curtain on the window sill, so that's where he went, still yowling. I got him into the cage, and took them both to the vet who was looking after them while the move happened, and Arthur didn't stop crying at all.

I picked them up in the afternoon, took them to the new flat (which is a very light first-floor flat as opposed to a dark basement, which the other one was), and let them out on the bed. They both ran straight underneath it, and I put food and water in the room with them and left the door open. In about half an hour Freya came out and started looking round; if I got up she'd run back under the bed, but as long as I was still, she'd explore. She then lay in the sun in the living room, and started stretching and cleaning herself. I got down at the side of the bed and Arthur came and sniffed my hand, and I saw he was shaking. Basically he stayed either under the bed or under the duvet for the next four days, only on one or two occasions going under the duvet – I think he felt more secure in the dark. I put down poached fish, cooked liver and cooked steak for him, but he would not eat anything. After four days, my knees were in agony from spending so much time kneeling on the wooden floor with him. So I brought him into the sitting room, put cushions under the sofa and chairs so he couldn't hide, and shut the door and stayed in there with him for a couple of hours. As soon as I opened the door he ran back under the bed, but that night he went back into the sitting room, and from then on he gradually started exploring. It took almost two weeks before I came home and he behaved 'normally'.

The other problem during this time is that Freya kept hissing at him, maybe she could smell the vet on him still, or maybe she just knew he was vulnerable. Anyway, it made me really

cross with her, but there wasn't a
lot I could do.

It was hard getting him eating
properly again, and it's weird, but
in the mornings when I'm getting ready
to go to work, he still won't come
anywhere near me, he hides under the
coffee table in the sitting room.

Hope it gets better with yours soon
- it's really worrying when they are
so upset.

Elspeth xx

Not content with pestering my sister and also Elspeth,
I then moan on to my long-suffering agent Kate, saying
never was there a disappearing cat who was so perplex-
ing as Pushkin, and she then sends me this wonderful
account from her husband Charles Carroll about the
introduction of a new Siamese whom they name Catastrophe into their household – which at this time
consists of themselves, their three-year-old daughter, and
a Tonkinese called Calamity. It is great therapy for me
to read this:

Generally [when introducing new cats to the household] we put the box on the floor, open the door, and wait for the newcomer to emerge inquisitive and eager to explore his new surroundings. And so we waited. And waited. Then we lost patience and gave him a little encouragement . . . His exit from the box would be familiar to anyone who has seen pictures of a Pershing missile launching from a nuclear silo. He shot across the kitchen floor, rose several feet in the air, bounced off the microwave and landed on a work surface before realising he was in a corner with nowhere to hide. In a textbook display of what *not* to do, I lunged after him – a gesture he clearly misunderstood – and ten seconds later he was behind the oven. I turned to Kate: 'Are they meant to do that?' . . . The following morning we looked behind the cooker and – horrors – he'd disappeared.

Most of day two was spent with mounting panic searching for the new hiding place. Needless to say, underneath the bathroom floor was

not the first place we thought of looking . . . In fact, it was only as I threw my socks in the laundry basket at the end of the day that I saw the small gap where one floorboard fails to meet the wall. I put my socks back on and went to find a torch. There is no dignity involved in searching for a missing cat. I grovelled on the floor with the torch in one hand and a mirror in the other, trying to reflect light round a corner . . . Just out of arm's reach a pair of red eyes stared back. It would be going too far to say that they looked smug, but something about the situation told me that the cat had the upper paw. I might have had control of the food and water supplies, but the eyes said, 'I've only got to do one poo down here and you'll have to take up the whole floor.'

I tried to tempt him out with food, I tried to drag him out by force, I even thought about trying to starve him out, but in the end I went to bed. Twenty minutes later I was asleep and he popped out for a snack.

This went on for the next three weeks. Every night he would wait until he was sure everyone was asleep, and then he'd creep out for a bite to eat before crawling back under the floorboards at first light. Eventually in desperation I pretended to be asleep and . . . while he was downstairs I whipped out a screwdriver and closed the hole. His new home was under the bed. This was an enormous step forward. Now we could see our new cat without lying on the bathroom floor with a mirror . . . But he became adept at staying hidden . . . Christmas came and went, and then one morning in January we were woken by a yowl from under the bed. After four months, two weeks and three days, our cat had spoken to us!

We jumped out of bed. He hid.

Catastrophe's reluctance to join the household continues, but all's well in the end, even if, in the course of his burgeoning self-confidence, he does, among other things, teach Calamity how to rip up the stair carpet.

'And finally,' Charles concludes 'if you do happen to find yourself with a Siamese trapped under the bathroom floor, try reading it *The Three Little Pigs* – they seem to like it.'

And the final word from friends on the subject of moving house and cats comes in these extracts from Karin Slaughter, who rather spectacularly decided on impulse, just driving round after shopping one day, that the house in front of her was the one she wanted; she fell in love with it and went for it and, hey presto, the big move was on!

The cats are getting settled into the new house, though Pete has been hiding in the master bedroom closet a lot. Workers have still been in and out and he's a scaredy cat, as you know. Sophie has been the real problem. We have a motion detector switch on one of the downstairs lights by the garage entrance and she keeps walking back and forth, swishing her tail, running down the batteries. I swear she is doing it on purpose, and it was so scary the first night when she did it because I thought someone had turned on the light so they could come up the stairs and rape us!

Love K xx

So I conclude from all of this that moving cats is definitely not a good thing in the short term, however good it may turn out to be in the long term. And I have learned – oh, *how* I have learned – never, for whatever reason, attempt to move with your cats into an empty house and then continue to live in it, with them, while it remains empty. No, Sir!

CHAPTER 16

We have served our sentence, and for all manner of reasons the time has come to return to the South. John has now returned to his parish in Scotland following his hard-earned and, in the event, hard-working holiday, but, remarkably, because he still has a little holiday in hand, he offers to come back to toil some more when next we are in residence at The Old Coach House.

A couple of days after John's departure, Michael and I both drive off south in our separate cars and yet again I take the cats in mine. Pushkin buries himself deep in the car and I am unable to see or hear him, but sadly I can smell him, as he is quite ill on this return journey.

Fannie complains loudly on and off at different points in the journey, and walks up and down the back of the car like a caged tiger. Titus just groans a bit and tries to sleep. On our entry into Moon Cottage, however, something astonishing happens. I lift Pushkin, shivering and shaking, out of the car, from deep under the blankets and a towel where he has been hiding, partially encrusted in his own excretions because he was too scared to move when he was ill, and I gently place him on the sitting room floor just inside the front door.

To begin with he just sits down and does some frantic grooming, but as I watch him, having addressed his immediate needs, he turns his head around and sniffs the air. He stands up and stretches – tall and proud – and then trots, with

unmistakable delight, through to the dining room, into the kitchen, and even out into the yard. I hold the door open and he races back inside and, as I follow with bags from the car, he bounds upstairs leaping joyfully two stairs at a time, straight into our bedroom and up on to the bed. He sniffs around and then off he hurtles downstairs again. He is holding his head high, and whacking his tail forcefully back and forth, which is what he does when all's right with the world. Titus, who is standing in the kitchen waiting impatiently for food to appear and who is travel worn and on edge, looks aghast as she is knocked sideways by a full jubilant head butt from Pushkin. I am taken aback. I didn't expect such an extraordinary transformation. Of course, I hoped he would be happier now in familiar territory with all the furniture and the hiding places and the things he loves around him, but I didn't expect his gratification to be *instant*. It somehow makes me feel even more remorseful. Titus and Fannie too, as soon as they have refuelled, are clearly happy and at ease to be back in the house where they were in fact born, but their apparent appreciation of it seems more modulated, but then I reckon that they *didn't* hate The Old Coach House; they were just slightly on edge there.

We have come back to pack up everything for the big

move, the real thing, for our future life in Cumbria, and to make sure that everything is in order for the rent or sale of the cottage, as it is on the market for both, but before we embark on that there is a great treat in store for me.

I am accompanying my friend Sue to collect a long-awaited Devon Rex girl from her breeder Heather Boucher* in Swanley. We arrive at Heather's place and I cannot believe the kitten feast that greets us inside the house. There are, it seems to me, Devon Rex kittens everywhere we look; they are lying in heaps, in piles, stretched out, curled up, suckling, purring, playing and rampaging. When I ask Heather about them she laughs and says one of her friends comes round regularly just for a breath of what she calls 'Devon Heaven'. The girl, Georgie, whom Sue is about to whisk off home, is in colour not unlike

---

* http://www.jonscottdevonrex.co.uk

Pushkin, a light smoky blue, but in looks she is her own creature completely. She has enormous bat-like ears and startling green eyes which seem to hold the eyes of whichever human is in front of her with unusual intensity – as with all Devon Rexes, she has a slightly other-worldly look to her and I fall completely and totally in love with her darling triangular face; the top of her head is the broadest wedge in the world, honing down to a tiny delicate pointed chin. She is rather dauntingly posh, I then discover, as her mother, who everybody calls Molly, is in reality Grand Champion Grizabella Ohbladi Ohblada. Molly is a beautiful black smoke colour with a jet-black triangular face. Georgie's dad is also a champ called Xenomorph Stuart Little, who, from his picture, I judge to be a creamy apricot, but to my inexpert eyes Georgie takes after her mother.

Heather says that there are usually two batches of Devon Rex kittens a year 'available for sale to people with nerves of steel and no valuable antiques'. Sue has long tried to convert me to the heaven of 'Devon', but I have resisted because they are so alert and hyperactive and I am simply not sure I am up to the challenge of it, but today, just today, I waver. Eventually we tear ourselves away and make the journey home to deliver Georgie to her new quarters where she is to meet for the first time her new live-in companions.

The first she meets as she enters the door is young Max, a handsome neutered tom Si-Rex, cream in colour with darker points, who is now coming up to five years old. He takes one look at her and runs. And then her next introduction is to the two venerable old ladies, Siamese siblings, called Chatto and Johnny, who are now twenty years old.

Sue deliciously calls all her cats after the names of publishers who have always had a certain literary brio, so she has had in her stable Spotti* (Eyre & Spottis-woode), Norah (Smallwood and, in a feline context, the mother of Chatto and Johnny, but not in the world of publishing!), Chatto (& Windus), Jonathan (Cape), Max (Reinhardt), and now Georgie (George Weidenfeld). As one who calls my best ginger girl Titus, I can only applaud Sue's complete disregard for the

---

* And before I knew her, a cat called Eyre too.

niceties of gender. While I am there, the two 'maiden aunts' initially seem to accept Georgie with a philosophical resignation that I recognise as the way of the older cat. After watching the adorable Georgie settle in quite happily, I quietly sneak off back to Moon Cottage to let Sue have that all-important bonding session with her feline family.

The following are edited updates on Georgie:

From:	Sue
To:	Marilyn
Sent:	Monday, 10 May, 17:31
Subject:	Re: Hello and Sunday

Marilyn
   Well, day two, and at the moment she is conked out, rolled up in my T-shirt fast asleep. There have been some hefty play sessions today, none of the expensive cat toys of course, but a drinking straw and the perennial favourite, plastic packing tape. A favourite of Max as well, so he sort of joined in for a rather formal game. As she's dashing about, he keeps track

and has done a fair amount of walloping, but equally, brave thing that she is, has biffed him back, they look like David and Goliath together, I must say. I think they are going to be friends, poor old Max misses all the fuss as the previous baby of the house, so I have been praising him like mad when he's been playing with her.

There was a bit of awkwardness going to bed. I left the hall light on to avoid any collisions in the dark, Johnny and Chatto had possession of the bed, and were hissing fit to bust as she gamely tried to climb up too, but they gave up in disgust and she spent the night under the duvet.

Otherwise it has got less fraught, they are not arguing among themselves much at all, and haven't turned their collective backs on me either, which is a good sign.

That she has settled in so quickly is extraordinary, she seems little fazed by all the spitting and swearing and, at one time, when Johnny was sitting on the arm of the chair,

```
hissing like a steam engine, she just
fell asleep. As you saw, she is such
a loving little thing, with a lovely
vocabulary of chirrups and tiny mews,
hisses and growlings. Quite gorgeous
and I waste endless amounts of time
just watching and playing with her
and trying to get her to stop tap-
dancing on the keyboard.
  Anyway, gone on too long altogether!
  See you soon.
  Love Sue


 -------------------
```

And then I receive this further update from Sue in the form of a letter, enclosing wonderful photos of Georgie.

Tunbridge Wells, 24 June

Dear Marilyn

Georgie is on my lap at the moment, on her back, playing with the telephone wire. She is rather damp round the nether regions, having fallen in the bath earlier, but my presence in the bath spared her full immersion. Her appetite continues unabated, she is so like that lamb on *Wallace and Gromit*. I am able to feed her all the varieties that make the others turn their noses up. This morning she had Swordfish in Mediterranean Sauce!

She is much brighter than the others. If you throw one of the paper balls down the back of the armchair, Max goes to the top of the chair and looks down mournfully, whereas Georgie takes a look, jumps down, and goes round the side and under the chair and gets it; quite a lot of brain processing for such a tiny creature. She is still an excellent retriever, and if in the middle of a game I get up and move around, there she is following behind with her piece of paper ready for it to be thrown again. This has had an effect on Max. He has started fetching things, which he rarely did before, other than his piece of string. But he doesn't follow through. Georgie's other favourite thing is bendy drinking straws, and again Max has started playing with those too.

They are still playing around – having enormous play fights, which I pray won't turn nasty when she gets bigger. Even now he still seems to come off worse, his poor neck has grazes where she has biffed him.

Chatto [who has chronic kidney disease] has been back to the vet again. We tried another type of kidney food preparation and she won't eat that either, so, as agreed, I am feeding her tuna every day – she eats that and has put on weight again. It also seems to stimulate her interest in food and she eats more chicken and so on as well now, so a respite, hopefully. She's due for another test in two months' time, so we will see then, but it's a case of keeping as well as possible for as long as possible now.

And then a little later, after a small gap, I get the following emails:

Marilyn

We're all fine here, Chatto is carrying on, I am feeding her with whatever she wants; she has terrible poo problems, but with the aid of buckets of air freshener I put up with it; poor lamb, nothing can be done about that either apparently. Still her weight keeps on an even keel for now. As for Georgie, I am scarred all over, she is a leaper, up me, up the curtains, up anything really, but for me, having flesh, it is particularly painful and of course looks awful – as if I have been lashing myself with barbed wire; but she's so quick, the words 'George, don't do that', which should of course be intoned in the right Grenfellian manner, come too late. We play umpteen games of fetch the paper ball a day, and it is very cross-making (poor

Georgie) when I am in the middle of work to see her come gambolling up with her paper ball in her mouth ready for a game or three. She is very loving at around 4 a.m., just when you don't want your chin and arms kneaded and drooled over, and my chest comes in useful as a perch when I am sitting reading. She's very smart and I love watching her work things out and learn from her mistakes. Poor Max still gets the worst of it, and he is becoming a bit of an Eeyore, very fatalistic and he is scratched as well! At the moment she is amusing herself playing with a ball in a great swathe of brown-paper packing material courtesy of Bloomsbury. And how she's grown, still fine boned and delicate, but her legs have ratcheted up, still too small to leap on the kitchen counter alas (which is where I, the human ladder, come in).

God damn it, Georgie just leapt on the keyboard and I've lost para- graphs . . . I can't remember what I wrote now, but I know I would love to see you and should be able to squeeze out some holiday soon. I am very envious [hearing from you about] the bird life surrounding your new house, I got excited yesterday just because I saw a sparrow and a butterfly and today a lapwing . . . much love from the town!

Sue

From:	Sue
To:	Marilyn
Sent:	Monday, 9 August, 20:12
Subject:	Re: Moon Cottage and the transition to The Old Coach House

Marilyn

Am now less blood-stained as Georgie is just big enough to get on the kitchen counter unaided. First it was the fridge, then the sink, then the extra inch for the counter . . . I am healing nicely. Her fur is just getting long enough to start curling; she is so gorgeous to look at. I doubt if Rexes are any cleverer than other cats, I think they are just more curious and this leads them into more learning (and trouble). You can't

do anything without her getting involved. I shall have to get her a clipboard...so she can oversee things properly.
  Hope you and Michael are well?
  Love
  Sue

And then, much later on, because both Sue and I have been submerged in work, so she never did make her holiday, I receive the following message:

From:	Sue
To:	Marilyn
Sent:	Tuesday, 19 October, 17:06
Subject:	Calamity

Marilyn
  Big turning point on Thursday, Georgie goes for her op [neutering] – will warn vet to put her first on the list or he will be driven to distraction by her wails at being ignored for more than two minutes. Like you, I was having fantasies about gorgeous

203

little grey kittens but, as have promised not to and it is entirely unpractical, will trudge down the vets come Thursday. What a quiet day that's going to be, no typing three words and throwing a piece of paper, no trooping across the keyboard, no dive bombing, able to answer the telephone without interference, no spillages, no excavations of bin, no collapse of piles of manuscripts, I shall be down the vet's well before pick-up time suffering from withdrawal symptoms.

All my love
Sue

From:	Sue
To:	Marilyn
Sent:	Tuesday, 26 October, 16:42

Georgie is fine, just had a chicken supper and is now chilling out on top of the computer, has left her stitches well alone and all is healing nicely; one or two spats with Max when I have feared for her wound, but no need for Casualty yet. We did have a drama on

Sunday when, as per usual, she helped
herself to some salad [she likes
mayonnaise] and shortly afterwards
starting wheezing like a grampus and
gulping and snorting. Just as we were
getting to the stage of having to get
the vet out [late on a Sunday night]
it all went away, so am presuming it
was watercress or black pepper that
set her off.

On Monday, however, Georgie and
Johnny were stretched out on the
mantelpiece (my having obligingly
moved the clock, candlesticks, etc.
up one end, so symmetry not to be
found here), and Johnny stretched and
by accident kicked Georgie, who was
fast asleep, sending her crashing down
on to the coffee table, where there
was an ashtray, full glass of water,
etc. Less worried about the mess than
the cat with only three lives left,
but she seemed fine and was soon as
perky as ever and no glass broken,
thank heavens. Am also now having to
forsake wicker waste bins for horrid
plastic ones with lids due to the
activities of the bin raider, and as

for artistic piles of loo-rolls – all
disembowelled; loo looked like I had
had an internal blizzard this morning.

Can only hope your cat population
is better behaved, and as for breeds,
still can't tempt you with a Rex?

Love Sue

CHAPTER 17

We start the preparations in earnest for the move, and we have asked the removal company to pack us up as we lack both time and space and also, truth to tell, I just can't face it! The plan of action is that Michael starts sorting out at the Moon Cottage end, while I return to Hutton Roof to get as much painting and decorating done as possible before the furniture comes in; Michael will commute back and forth, but this time we will leave the cats in Moon Cottage. Johnny has now moved back into Moon Cottage in order to get his things organised for his own move into his little cottage down the road, which is to happen at the same time as our move, so he has offered to do any requisite cat-sitting in the meantime.

Stephen is coming up to Hutton Roof to help us do all that we need to do, and it is agreed that he will be in charge of operations – any of us who are around will be his 'go-fers'. The big idea is that we finish stripping the paper off all the walls, make good the surfaces, and get the rooms painted before the carpets go down. Now, without the cats here, we are free to do any amount of hammering, sawing and other destructive manoeuvres that cats loathe, as well as being able to leave doors and windows wide open. So as Stephen comes up from the South, and John approaches down from the North, The Old Coach House prepares to rock.

The reason we have embarked on the major redecoration is that as we strip off the initial wallpaper, Stephen, our decorating mentor, explains to us that we mustn't just slap paint over the old paper underneath, as it will simply peel off again within a year. This will almost certainly be why every room has been papered over and over again by successive owners (because the painting option was too problematic) and now the stripping-down becomes almost archaeological as the papers get older and stranger in colour and texture. The house slowly begins to reveal to us a small hint of its history as we delve into its many skins. To begin with, the house, in all its parts, had an elegant, feminine feel to it. But, as we strip back the walls in the older part of it – the original coach house – the combination of dark colours that emerge in those rooms suggests that successive masculine hands have been at work. As we labour in our separate rooms, on our allotted projects, we each get to know the house and its character more intimately.

For the first few nights John is with us, but when his 'holiday' runs out he has to return to Scotland. Each weekend Michael comes up, and in between times it is just Stephen and me. Stephen, in a uniquely tactful way, is a hard taskmaster, and he himself works astoundingly long hours, so there are many nights when he doesn't knock off until midnight. Each night, around 10 p.m., we 'open the bar' – which means uncorking a bottle of wine or opening up a bottle of beer – and that is when we wind down and talk.

One evening Stephen, who is a smoker, goes out into

the garden for his ciggie and when he comes back inside he observes casually:

'That's a really lovely cat that was sitting up on the wall, and he looks really big.'

'What cat, Stephen? I never saw him.'

'Come on, you'll see.' Michael and I go rushing out, but he has run off. But later on that night, Michael sees him too.

'What does he look like?' I plead.

'He is mainly black in the body, but he has a white face and white front and white paws. He's a stunner.'

'Why do you keep saying "he"? Could be "she" just as easily.'

'No, not that large, definitely "he"!' Michael insists. I keep looking out for 'their' cat, but I fail to see him.

My role develops, by default, as that of chief cook and bottle washer, acquirer of paint, brushes, sandpaper, sealant, tiles, trim, turpentine, dustsheets, ladders, etc., and part-time scraper, sander and painter. The clock, of course, is ticking against us, as the time approaches for the great move. Stephen, in particular, works longer and longer hours and, by dint of sheer graft, the 'to do' list is showing an encouraging array of ticks. On the very last night, Stephen and I carry on painting, almost frenziedly, in order to get as much done as possible and it is well past midnight when I finally persuade him to put down his brush and eat some food. In the spirit of a job well done, we open another bottle after that first bottle, and start to put the world to rights – leaving only the smallest pebbles unturned. I go out into the conservatory to use the lavatory, and as I glance through the window I see a violet streak of light arcing across the sky, which momentarily puzzles me, but as I open the door I hear a couple of tentative trills of birdsong and I leap back inside and call Stephen out.

As he joins me outside, the two or three bird voices have now increased to at least five or six, and then suddenly they have multiplied tenfold into the full-blooded glorious but (if you have not yet gone to bed) terrifying sound of the *dawn* chorus. As we walk across the garden to the hedge on the far side and look out over the dark majestic hills of Yorkshire still enfolded in the shadow of night, the violet streak grows in front of our eyes into a broad pink glow which dramatically silhouettes the hills and, as we watch, transfixed, the sun climbs slowly up the sky, turning everything it touches into pure gold. It is a perfect sunrise. My eyes fill with tears and I feel a pleasure so intense that it makes my chest tighten in pain, but fortunately just at that moment Stephen starts to tell me something really important in a worryingly loud voice, and my doubtless misplaced fear that we will awaken our newly acquired neighbours (their house is, after all, several hundred feet away) at this antisocial hour obliterates all else as I try to shut him up. He misunderstands what is concerning me and I don't want to speak loudly, so instead, attempting to muffle our by now hysterical laughter, I hastily shepherd us back into the house where, exhausted, we retire to our beds to get what sleep we might.

The following day Stephen kindly volunteers to finish clearing up and closing down the house behind me while I drive off to Michael's farewell-from-the-office party in London – and what a send-off that is. People from the whole of his working life, some of whom he has not seen for many a year, come to that party. He will be much missed, and I am proud for him that he now truly begins to know just how much. Michael and I get back to Moon Cottage late that night, and from then on we find ourselves running on yet another 'to do' treadmill that is moving ever faster. The move is to take place over five days – two packing, one loading, one driving, and one unloading at the other end.

Although I try to keep the cats contained and out of the way as much as possible, it is quite evident to all three of them that *bad things are happening*. Strange men with large boxes and endless wrapping paper keep coming and going and it does not bode well, and of course I feel guilty because I can't explain what's going on. In the end the packing takes three days, and on our last day all three of us go into the garden and say our farewells, but in a rather rushed way, and because the cottage is not yet sold, we know that we, if not the cats, will be back again.

On the third day, Moon Cottage is finally completely empty but for a small sofabed that no one wanted in the sitting room, and Johnny and his friend, Al, who is lodging with him and therefore helping to pay off some of the mortgage on his cottage, lie on it like replete

Roman emperors in a mock debauched farewell to see us off. They have already moved themselves into their cottage and are smugly grinning as they know what lies ahead of us on a more epic scale. Michael, who is one big softie, gets tearful and we all have to be very jolly indeed to stop him having a big old blub. (We had had an emotional farewell dinner with Johnny earlier in the week, at which we had all repeatedly reassured ourselves that all three boys, Johnny, Ollie and Damian, would be making regular visits to Cumbria and that we were not going to a remote inaccessible island that no one had ever heard of, and all of them would be coming up and down like yo-yos.)

Right in the middle of our huge 'joviality', the doorbell goes and it is a man from the depot opposite with a bottle of champagne scrunched up in a Tesco's bag to say they will all miss us; emotionally, this really is the terminal straw on the poor old camel's back as it is so completely unexpected. Shirley and Stephen and Karen and Mark had all come round and wished us a proper farewell a couple of nights earlier and that was painfully sad, as it was when we said goodbye to Eve and John from nearby Stocker's Lock, which is where Beetle, the brother of Fannie and Titus, lives too. It was pretty terrible saying goodbye to Father Jim, the priest who received me into the Catholic Church and who, together with John, Michael's brother, solemnised the marriage between Michael and me, and whom I adore (although he never lets you tell him that), and also the community within the church who have been so welcoming. The combination of all of these things makes us wonder why we are doing it all, and then suddenly it is all over and we are off; we pile the cats into the back of my car (of course!), and all the luggage and heavy stuff into Michael's car, and off we set.

When we arrive at The Old Coach House I reckon that the one room that is likely to remain off limits to the removal men will be the bathroom with the Juliet balcony, and so I collect together all the cat bedding and the food and water and cat litter trays, together with the three cats, and shut them all in there and pray. There is a small wardrobe in the bathroom and instantly Pushkin wriggles himself under the blanket on the floor of the wardrobe and doesn't budge, but as it is dry and clean and warm – unlike his hole under the stairs or, worse still, the pipes behind the sink – I leave him be. Fannie, predictably, jumps up on to the top of the wardrobe, so I find a small duvet and fold it up as bedding for her, and from here she surveys her small tiled empire. Titus looks around resignedly and, sighing, flops down on to her duvet cushion on the floor. And for the moment that is where they rest.

After the removal men finally clang shut the rear ramps of their two huge wagons and depart, Michael and I look at each other and groan. It is wonderful that they pack you up, but of course they can't unpack you; and when they have packed you, even though they write 'kitchen' on the box, it isn't necessarily certain that you would want all your bathroom gear in the kitchen, so opening each box is something of a lottery. The whole house, with the exception of the bathroom with the cats in it, is a wall-to-wall mountain of boxes and bags and cases.

'Remind me *never, ever* to move house again!' Michael says as he stoically sets about unpacking. He is tireless and shames me as I give up too easily, but between us the house begins to take shape and look like home surprisingly quickly, although in truth it is weeks before we get the final packing case open. I leave the cats in the bathroom overnight, but Michael and I, who are at this stage sleeping on a mattress on the floor of the adjoining bedroom, are well within earshot and they stay still and calm, surprisingly, the whole night through. In the morning we open the bathroom door and let them free. Fannie and Titus come out and are overjoyed to find the familiar furniture with all their smells on it, but Pushkin will not budge. For the next few hours I keep hearing Fannie and Titus scratching every single bit of furniture they can find as they do their territorial marking, and they jump up and down off every sofa, every packing case; we have mattresses propped up at weird angles, and if they can find a nook and cranny to hide within and spring out at each other, then they do.

Fannie in particular, even though a fully adult matron now, is a liability. She loves getting into things. Plastic bags with duvets rolled up are her favourite, but anything resembling them will do. Both the girls are nervous and jumpy, and if either of us drops anything in the epic unpacking they instantly run for cover, but they are also curious and the presence of familiar furniture makes such a difference.

For five days now I haven't been able to get Pushkin to move out of the bathroom; I carry him out, but he simply slinks on his stomach straight back in again. I had talked to Margot earlier about the pheromone that Jacqueline had mentioned in her email that, and Margot now tells me that she used a dog pheromone for Snowy, her Westie, when they moved into their new house. It had helped, and she urges me to get some. I am not yet registered with a local vet, so she kindly offers to get some from her own vet.

Seven days after we have moved, the cat pheromone arrives in the post. The magical elixir is called Feliway and it arrives complete with an electric diffuser. In other words, it comes with a plug-in contraption, rather like one of those mosquito repellents or air fresheners, and the significant ingredient within it appears to be 'a synthetic analogue of the F3 fraction of feline facial pheromone', which apparently has a calming effect on stressed cats. But the extraordinary thing is – it does! It works. I cannot believe it, but it really does work. I plug it into the bathroom and two days later Pushkin decides he is feeling brave enough to venture downstairs. He comes down, blinking a little, and looks around him. He climbs on a few things and then jumps down again and rubs his cheeks against everything in sight, repeatedly and as high as possible. It is as if he has been in a deep sleep and now he has at last awoken. For several days past I have been letting Titus and Fannie out into the garden, and Michael, by gently throwing fir cones at them when he wants them to come back inside, has 'trained' them to come in on the shout of a bellowed couple of 'In, In'.

When Pushkin comes down, the front door is open

and he can see that the girls are outside, and to my delight he tiptoes out and nervously joins them. He sits down and looks all around him, in wonder. Just then a tractor comes up the hill; he panics at the noise and runs back inside, but it is a wonderful start all the same. I leave the Feliway plugged into the bathroom for several more weeks, but eventually I feel it has done its job and unplug it. Pushkin has now properly joined the rest of the household and our new life can begin.

CHAPTER 18

While all this has been going on my brother-in-law, Rod, in America, has been dying, and my sister, Judy, has bravely and stoically nursed him at home for the entire span of his illness, with only the briefest interludes of hospitalisation. It is now evident, though, that he will not live for very much longer. Their children, Mark, Claire and Emma, are at home with Judy and Rod, as it is Rod's wish that home is where he would prefer to die. Margot, my other sister, has flown out to be with them, and although I long to go, Judy feels she has more than enough on her plate with all that is going on without another body filling up the place.

Very soon after Margot has left, however, I get the expected news that Rod has died; so I fly out to Texas for the funeral, leaving Michael at home to cat-sit. One of the hardest things in the world is watching loved family members suffering grief. There is something so wretched about the sight of broken hearts, and there is so little than can be done to mend them; and time, most cruelly, takes its *time*. None of them has a cat either, and I believe cats help so much when you are hurting.

Meanwhile, the news from Moon Cottage – or, more to the point, the absence of news from Moon Cottage – begins to ring alarm bells. In May, the Governor of the Bank of England had issued a statement urging people not to invest their money in property and it had an immediate effect on the house market, slowing it right down. Now, in June, the Bank of England has raised interest rates, which of course has a knock-on effect on mortgage rates, and the market in the south of England just goes static. We have not had any more viewings, so we change agents. When we are *still* without viewings, I begin to fear exactly what this might mean long term.

One morning, soon after I get back from America, Michael and I sit down at The Old Coach House and have a conversation that even two weeks ago I would not have believed possible.

'If this goes on, you do realise that we will have to try and sell up here and go back down.'

'Michael, you cannot mean this. Not after all that we have done up here!'

'I don't want this any more than you, but we simply don't have the money to go on, and we must rent or sell one or the other.' We both look out of the window at paradise, then at each other, and the overwhelming sense of sorrow is terrible. Shortly after this, Geoffrey comes to visit us and his response is: 'Listen, in a crisis keep your eye on the big picture; this house is the big picture, believe me.' Michael and I hold on to his words like a life raft.

Midsummer's day has just passed and it is raining fit to bust. Tonight we have lit a fire, although Michael complains it is far too warm for fires – which it probably is. The time is eight minutes past eleven and it is still glowing light in the garden; there is a raucous blackbird on the telephone wire outside with a long worm in its beak, tail flicking and wings flapping, going 'chink . . . chink . . . chink . . .' on and on and on. And soon that noisy pair of tawny owls will start. All night long they make their hunting calls, not so much the hoo-oo-oo-oo that everyone associates with them, but more raucously 'kee-wick, kee-wick, kee-wick' as persistently as the male blackbird has just been making his chink-chink sound. Annabel tells me that they are teaching their young to hunt, and in fact I now remember that owlets leave the nest long before they can fly and the parents spend long hours at night time feeding them up; and from the sound of it, they are about five yards outside our bedroom window.

This place is astonishingly rich in the variety of its birdlife; it is like nowhere I have ever lived. It is bird paradise right here with our tiny private forest of seven Scots pines and then the big woodland behind going up to the crags. It is as if we have landed on a desert island where no predator has ever been experienced. The birds come so close to us, they seem truly fearless. They group round the numerous feeders in the garden and come right up to the windowsills and peck at the windows with astounding bravura. Today in response to a new seed that I have just put out, there were numerous visits from several chaffinches, one crossbill showed himself, but not at the seed, up in the Scots pines, two greenfinches, four goldfinches, one chiffchaff or willow warbler (cannot tell the difference), and for the first time in my life knowingly I saw a yellowhammer. He came right up to my window and apparently winked at me. Earlier today I had had my first close-up of a great spotted woodpecker, and the richness of the colouring of the white and the scarlet was truly stunning. He banked at the feeding table, seemed to grab a beak full of seed, and shot off like a Red Arrow.

Although the cats were in the study with me, the two girls were asleep on the armchair behind me and missed it all, and Pushkin was in his posh bed under the chair, which is where he now seems to live. A permanent birdlife feature is the gathering around the hanging nuts and the giant fat balls, which regularly includes great tits, bluetits, coal tits and, wonderfully – as I have never seen them before – long-tailed tits, which is quite a turn-out. We have a pair of collared doves who sit on the wires outside my study window, day after day, and recently Michael found a fledgling, not obviously wounded, but certainly grounded, under a bush in our garden. We carefully moved it to a field across the road, so that none of the cats would find it, but today Michael made me follow him up the road.

'Look down there!' he points at the road.

'What? I can't see anything.'

'Yes you can – look closer.' And as I bend down I suddenly realise that horribly, almost like an X-ray, there is etched in the tarmac a perfect profile of a flat miniature-collared dove, so the little fledgling clearly got tractored.

Titus has started to be sick on a fairly regular basis and today she was sick several times. Michael and I have a mild spat about how many sicks ago each of us cleaned up, which results in the immortal assertion from Michael:

'The last time you cleaned it up, it was at least six sicks ago, I know it was!' So, quite rightly, I set to. I think it is pure greed on Titus's part rather than an illness, but, just in case, I take her down to our local vet, where I see Gerard, who is very charming and helpful. In fact, I take all three cats as they are due their injections. Gerard examines them all and I tell him about Titus's history with her dislocating knees. He thinks I probably should have her neutered, and I agree, although he understands that I would still like to have one litter from Fannie; he is surprised that no local toms have come a-calling. He is, as are all the other vets with whom I have discussed it, surprised that Pushkin has not performed, but presumes it is the multi-cat environment that is putting him off. He now thoroughly examines Titus and reckons she is not ailing, but suggests I use a special food for sensitive stomachs. When I try feeding it to her, though, she won't eat it; so we carry on with her usual food, Hill's, and with her being intermittently sick. Is feline bulimia a possibility, I wonder to myself, not entirely seriously?

Titus and Fannie both go out into the garden more regularly and stay out for longer. Titus goes into the field behind and spends hours eating grass, which no doubt adds to the likelihood of her being sick, and

Fannie climbs the garden shed and sits on the roof, although she is nervous if left out in the garden for too long. Pushkin, although he goes out, never stays out long and the moment he hears any vehicle coming up the road he leaps inside again. He is now sleeping regularly on the chair in my study, which has hitherto been the terrain of the girls, so there is a bit of a territorial battle going on here. Cats and their chosen resting places are a mystery. One place will remain a favourite for a long time and then suddenly, for no apparent reason, it goes out of favour and an alternative snoozing place is found. And because another cat might take the place that has been vacated, the explanation can-

not simply be that now it is, say, suddenly draughty.

As each day goes by, all three cats are more visibly relaxed, and are moving further afield as they go out, so I live in permanent fear of the road. The gate, which is now hung properly, does seem to be doing its job of deterrence, this in spite of Titus, who looks longingly through the bottom of it when she first comes out of the front door. Pushkin has, three times, jumped up and sat on top of it, in a frenzy of indecision as to whether to jump down into the road or not. Fannie's greatest area of vulnerability is the tall garden wall that is the shared boundary between us and the Old Vicarage next door, as that has twice been her chosen way of exit.

Having watched Titus, they have all started to go into

the field at the back where they chew grass and then panic when they hear a dog either being walked by a nearby neighbour or playing with one of the campers. Fannie, as well as climbing the shed, also sometimes climbs up the trunk of the nearest of the seven Scots pines, but they are so very tall that she gives up at around twenty feet and backs down. Today she is very quietly and studiedly looking into the pond, and because none of the cats has yet made an attempt to kill either the fish or the frogs neither Michael nor I are paying full attention. There is suddenly a loud splash and I hear gales of laughter from Michael.

'So how was your first swim, Fannie? Good, eh?' I see Fannie streak wetly into the hallway and round into her favourite chair in the conservatory where she licks and licks until she is dry. Soon, within half an hour, Pushkin does the identical thing. Titus alone resists the temptation.

Thomas and Doreen, our Dales friends, come over for supper one evening, and although when we were house hunting they were lobbying for us to live nearer Wensleydale, they are very gracious about how utterly lovely it is in this long summer twilight on the Cumbrian side of the hills. Rather magnificently while they are here, the tawny owls sit obligingly on the telephone wires, making the odd swoop into the field opposite our window, and Doreen reckons that the owls make it the perfect evening. I subsequently discover, however, that an owlet was wounded and grounded down in the field opposite and it was rescued by some local children, and Ian, who owns the field, had to get the local wildfowl trust to take it away to their clinic where they hope to mend its broken wing. If it survives, then it will be brought back and released. Meanwhile, for two nights the parent owls make the most terrible fuss, as they 'grieve' for their little one and try to find it.

Oliver comes to stay for a few days and it is wonderful to see him. He is fit and well and I am struck at how handsome a young man he has become; although he was always an angelic-looking boy, he is now a blond athletic-looking six-footer. Michael, Ollie and I go for a walk up the crags behind us, which is quite a haul, but the view from up there is breathtaking. It is possible on a clear day to see way over into Yorkshire looking east, the mountains of the Lake District proper looking north, and Morecambe Bay looking west. The great Wainwright* says:

> All roads to Hutton Roof lead uphill and the village is well named, lying along an elevated slope with far-reaching panoramas across the valley of the Lune ... the summit provides an outstanding distant prospect of range after range of mountain and fell to every point of the compass: a superb viewpoint.

We walk and talk, but eventually decide that we should return home. Michael claims he wants to go the 'direct' route home but, because I know the crag consists of treacherous limestone pavements with steep hidden edges and the bracken is way taller than any man so it is impossible once you leave a path to see where you are going, I declare that I'm descending via a footpath. Ollie

---

* *Westmorland Heritage* by A. Wainwright (Frances Lincoln).

is torn, as he has to decide which one of us he should accompany on the return journey. On balance, he decides that Michael is the one who is being the most irresponsible so therefore he is the one who needs accompanying, so we part company and I duly find the footpath and climb back down to the village and up to The Old Coach House. When I get there I have no house key as Michael has it, so I sit down in the garden and wait. And wait. And wait. I can see the cats through the window, but have no way of getting in. Also, I am frantically thirsty.

Eventually, after a further three-quarters of an hour, I hear Michael's and Ollie's voices, so I hide behind a bush by the hedge. When they get to the front door Michael is concerned that there is no sign of me and I continue hiding for as long as I can spin it out although, rather disgracefully, I am childishly pleased that he sounds so worried. In the end, though, my own thirst and a wish to put him out of his distress make me reveal myself. They had had to retrace their steps back to the summit as Michael had indeed led them to a sheer precipice and there was no getting down it, it turned out.

Shortly after this, Stephen returns to finish the one outstanding decorating job, the kitchen. One of the things that happens this time, as Stephen works his way around the kitchen, is that he starts to fall in love. All his life he has been a dog man, and he and Shirley adore Dante, their huge black labrador, who is virtually the size of a small Shetland pony; but Stephen has now become enraptured by the delicate girlie flirtatious charm of Fannie. Because Fannie has just that effect on me, I know full well how he feels. He becomes as keen as I am that she should have kittens to keep the line going and says he would love one. Sadly, he is allergic to cats, and when around them has to live on daily doses of antihistamines, so I am not sure it would work for him.

One evening as Michael, Stephen and I are all sitting in the garden quietly chatting, looking across at the awe-inspiring view, Stephen suddenly grips my arm:

'Look, look. Over there, there is the answer for Fannie.' As I look across I see a beautiful black and white cat perched on the top of the wall, watching us. He has penetrating green eyes and a jet-black crown

and ears, a dramatic black eye mask, a white nose and muzzle, and a white bib and legs. He is lovely. He would be a wonderful father for Fannie's kittens.

'Do you really think he is a tom?'

'Well, one way to find out is to leave Fannie out all night?'

'Ah, now I couldn't do that.' I get up to go and stroke the black and white cat and to try to see if he is a full tom, but as I approach him he jumps off the gate and runs off down the road towards the village centre. We see this beautiful cat just once more before Stephen leaves.

For the remainder of his stay Stephen works away like a Trojan. This time it is tougher and takes longer, as he has no helpers – on this occasion I am frantically writing and Michael is busy selling books. When Stephen finally leaves The Old Coach House I have the distinct feeling that, if not before, then certainly now it contains some part of his essence, just as Moon Cottage does too.

Shortly after Stephen returns south, I notice that the pair of collared doves is no longer a pair but now only one. One of them had in fact gone lame and the one that remains is not at all lame, so I conclude it was the lame one that finally met its end. I am sure that this one is the parent of the flattened chick we found in June, and although I do not think doves are mono-gamous, as are swans, I reckon they are pretty loyal to each other. This solitary one sits on the electric wire that runs parallel to my window and its singular condition depresses me.

Shirley, Stephen's mother, widowed out of the blue less than two years ago, and still acutely missing her soul mate John, comes up to see us and it is wonderful to have her here and show her all that Stephen has done, and also for her to get a real break from school – where she works – and a change of scenery. As she and I are sitting out in the conservatory, the solitary collared dove lands on the wire opposite and I tell her what has happened. I can feel the power of her empathy for it.

Shirley is one of the most generous bighearted people I have ever met, and it is wonderful to see her again and, as with Judy too, and many others, I ask that eternal question 'Why do bad things happen to good people?' While she is here she quickly develops a rapport with the three cats, even though I had hitherto got her down as a 'dog woman'. I often hear her calling Titus and Fannie and Pushkin with a real yearning. And Fannie and Titus both respond to her with warmth. (Pushkin remains wary, but he's Pushkin.) Every night that she is here, when she opens her door to go to the bathroom Fannie enters with her little whiney miaow in greeting.

Down at their cottage in Watford, Johnny and Alan suddenly find themselves looking after two kittens, who seem to have been abandoned. (This is an irony for

Johnny as he has always claimed that he is a 'dog man', and swore that once he had his own place he would immediately get himself a dog; but he, like all Michael's sons, is truly an 'animal' lover.) The kittens are only about eight weeks old apiece when they are first adopted and are called Duggers and Hammy, after each of the boy's surnames, but Johnny, who is hopelessly biased and whose surname begins with D, texts me the following info: 'Duggers is the nice caring one, Hammy is always on the tiles, still talking cats too!' Duggers is entirely black, and Hammy has a little white pattern on his chest. They are very cute, and I reckon that they can only be good news for these two lads who are now living in what could be the perfect set-up for 'men behaving badly'; the cats may induce in them a sense of responsibility! These two small cats become significant to our cats in Hutton Roof after a quick trip I make to Moon Cottage, however, during which Johnny brings me a computer box which is a present for Michael, and I duly cart it back north with me.

One day shortly after I am back at Hutton Roof I am standing in Michael's study when I hear a quiet but persistent hissing sound, like a very fine hydraulic hose, and as I turn round I see Pushkin just finishing spraying the bottom two shelves of Michael's signed first editions. I scream at him and he runs off quickly. To begin with I am mystified as he has never done this before and I cannot see any reason for it, but afterwards I realise that he was trying to hit the computer box and, being inexperienced, his aim is really bad. Michael reckons that Hammy and Duggers had each put their own marks on the box and Pushkin just felt compelled to cover it too. We both groan in fear that this is the beginning of a trend, but pray not!

CHAPTER 19

Most of July has been very wet and warm followed by an intensely hot and dry spell, which seems to have produced an unusual epidemic of wasps. It started even when Stephen was still with us and, as he hates them with a passion, his violent anti-wasp diatribes used to make me laugh. They were deliciously extreme.

Damian, Jo and baby Oskar come to stay and I am, as ever, utterly enchanted by Oskar. He is the sweetest-natured baby in the world; he almost never cries and he gurgles and laughs endlessly. Jo and Damian are both remarkably good parents and Damian has a real talent for calming Oskar and comforting him; and it is really nice to see how much he does towards the overall care of his small son. I am also moved at what a superb granddad Michael is.

I am concerned that all should be well for Oskar during his stay at The Old Coach House, being mindful that Damian and Jo are first-time parents and so might naturally be expected to be more apprehensive for their baby's safety than would be more seasoned baby-makers. So it's with some dismay that on the morning after their first night of this visit, I hear Damian calmly announcing:

'I just thought you should know that I have shut our bedroom window because the room was getting full of bees and Oskar is up there asleep at the moment.'

'When you say "full", do you mean just a couple?'

'No, I mean "full"; that is to say, there were lots. I didn't exactly count them – I just got rid of them and shut the window.' I look across at Michael, but he isn't paying any attention, so I go outside. To my horror, as I look up over the roof of the conservatory towards the room that Oskar is sleeping in, I see a hoard of bees flying distractedly in the air. It is hard to estimate the number, but well over fifty, probably closer to a hundred, and even to my inexpert eye they are clearly agitated. I rush inside and close all the windows and doors, but of course some have already got inside the house. Damian remains very calm and shrugs his shoulders. His view is if we simply keep everything shut, it will be fine. Michael and I go outside again and now we find that in the sloping roof vault over the downstairs lavatory, immediately under the tiles, there is a furious buzzing sound and bees are flying rapidly in and out. The number now looks greater.

'I reckon we've got a swarm, you know,' I anguish. Michael says:

'Don't worry, I'll go and get Richard.' We know that Richard and Annabel have newly taken to keeping bees and have several active hives. Richard comes and looks at the offending crack in the wall where they have been flying in and out, but there are not many to be seen now as they are all inside busy buzzing.

'They are probably all in there fanning the queen, as she will need to be kept cool,' he observes, matter-of-factly. He is uncertain that they are his bees, but I, on the other hand, am *absolutely* certain they are, because they are rather trim, pale-coloured bees and not like normal wild honey bees at all. I ask him about his bees and he says that his are partly Italian and are very hard workers, crossed with the indigenous black bee. He then goes off to seek advice from an apiarist friend. Soon after he has left, Annabel comes across and has a look too; I say to her I think that they might be Richard's bees, and she laughs conspiratorially and says she is sure I could be right.

I now spend hours on the phone trying to find a pest control person to come and destroy the bees and discover, when I can get through, which isn't often, that every pest controller within a radius of fifty miles is busy destroying wasps' nests. It has indeed been a season of wasp fecundity and every supermarket within miles has sold out of wasp-killer. When I eventually speak to a man from Environmental Health I discover that it is just as well for Richard's sake that I did not find any wasp-killer as the bees, who were probably a small breakaway group with a young surplus queen from Richard's hives, might have taken the poison back to the parent hive and killed the lot. The man gives me the name of a bee specialist who promises to come out in three days' time.

'*Three days*, but we can't breathe and all the windows are shut and the doors!'

'Really sorry, but I've never known a season like it for wasps, it is phenomenal; but if you make a lot of noise inside the area where they are they may move off – they may only be resting there!' I start to use the washing machine and put on the tumble drier in the little room that is immediately below the space where the bees are nesting, and we spend the rest of the day when we are in the house behind closed doors and windows.

That evening Richard reappears wanting an update on the bees, and as he and I stand outside the little window of the lavatory we discover, to my huge relief, that they seem to have gone. The following morning there is not a bee in sight, other than the normal bumble bees going about their daily business, so either they didn't like the heat or noise of a tumble drier, or they were indeed just resting while they made up their mind where to go. We never did know where they went, though.

Meanwhile Michael and I remain totally besotted with Oskar and spend hours drooling over him. The following day Jo and Damian lay him down on a blanket on the floor in the sitting room to kick his legs and as he gurgles away I carefully watch the cats. What is touching is that each of them in turn visits him and each very delicately smells the top of his head (why do babies' heads smell so wonderful?) and then quietly walks away. It makes me think of the reverencing of the Christ child by the shepherds and the wise men, and I recall with fondness that Christmas classic by Michael Foreman* in which the slightly sceptical cat never has the heart to catch a mouse again after his encounter with the 'shepherds with their bleating sheep, the rich men with their grumpy camels, even the man and the woman with their baby'. Eventually our little family of three wend their way back south, and we know with

---

* *Cat in the Manger* by Michael Foreman (Andersen Press, 2000).

sadness (for us) that they will ultimately go to live in Sweden, which is where Jo's family live.

This is not, however, the case with Fannie sadly – lacking the heart to kill a mouse that is, not move to Sweden. Her personal kill-toll in her new environment stands at three adult fieldmice, one baby fieldmouse with its eyes still shut, one tiny adult vole (and this is not taking into account those that Michael has rescued and released), and today all three of them did for a small adult bluetit who was foolish enough to fly into the conservatory through the bottom of the cat grill.

Pushkin has now, as a result, taken up the watch and is lolling on a chair by the open window waiting for more 'game' to come in. I think he thinks if he sits still long enough they will just fly into his mouth. In truth, given the number of birds we have here, one bluetit is a blessedly low death toll, but I am sorry that the cats are so fast off the ground with small mammals.

People in the village have been extraordinarily friendly and generous in the way they have welcomed us, and I feel guilty that we have not returned their hospitality; but for the moment we are battening down the hatches until we know where we stand with Moon Cottage. One of the many couples who have gone out of their way to welcome us are Ian and Elizabeth, who share their house with a beautiful tabby cat called Cathy, whom they otherwise call Little Puss. The one small thing I have been able to do for them in return, while they have been away in France, is to go down to their house every other day and give Cathy a tummy rub, a few strokes and a little companionship (although their immediate neighbours, Liz and Paul, are really looking after her).

Ian and Elizabeth are wonderful on the cat life, past and present, within the village of Hutton Roof. But on the here and now, I am curious to know why Little Puss is also called Cathy. Ian explains that there was a cat called Heathcliff, who everyone in the village reckoned belonged to them, although the couple who were properly his guardians were Ian and Cynthia. But anyway the real truth of it is that Heathcliff knew the village belonged to him, and this is simply how it was. Heathcliff, sometimes known as Liffy, was a big fluffy ginger cat with a white stomach and a punishing cry – 'wail, wail, wail' – which was usually rewarded by food or milk or other attention when he utilised it. One day, Heathcliff, mature lord-of-his-domain, turns up at Ian's and Elizabeth's door with a young female cat beside him (around five months old at this time they subsequently discover, but unusually tiny). Anyway, Heathcliff demands to come in, in his time-honoured fashion and, finding the door now open, in he trots escorting this young demure little creature. Without more ado, he takes her right round the cottage, downstairs, upstairs, almost no room is overlooked by the pair. Ian, as he is telling me this tale, is laughing:

'It was like "what's mine is yours, and this is one of mine" – he really was trying to impress her and he was doing a bloody good job, so as he was called Heathcliff, she had to be called Cathy.' And Cathy, naturally, interprets the whole thing as a formal invitation to join the household, so join it she does. She has a scar with stitches, so presumably she has been neutered recently by someone, but they never do find out who.

Heathcliff was in all sorts of ways a larger than life character, but not without soul. He had a really bad relationship with Hilary's cat at that time, one Toby, and the two of them used to have serious and recurring fights. Hilary and Phil live opposite Ian and Elizabeth, and it is Hilary who tells me this part of the tale. Toby became ill and eventually died. When he died, Hilary and Phil buried him in their garden near the side of the wall. She shows me where he is. To her amazement, and also Ian's too, who corroborates this story, Heathcliff sat on the wall staring down for hours at a time for three whole days following the death of his sparring partner, Toby. Who is to say whether it was grief, or triumph, or just plain missing?

Another remarkable story is illustrated by Peter Warner at the beginning of this chapter. In 1950 an aunt of Janet Bleay, who lives at a farm just across the field from The Old Coach House, bred Border Terriers in Otterburn in Northumberland, for which she had won many prizes, so each litter was highly coveted. Shortly before the photo that inspired Peter's sketch was taken, the bitch who had given birth to this litter had died, reason unknown, and Christabel, one of their house cats, who had herself just had a litter, had one kitten of her own remaining and so, doubtless full of her own maternal feelings and hearing the distress of the orphaned pups, she just crawled into the whelping box and suckled the pups herself, presumably in rotation.

CHAPTER 20

We have been letting all three cats out on a more regular basis and for longer chunks of time, but I find I remain very tense while the door remains open and they are outside. For a few days I had started to relax, feeling they were all calmly self-contained within the garden, until the morning dawned that sharply reminded me of their vulnerability. Titus likes to lie on the sun-warm tiles near the pond, with her tail slightly twitching, content enough to stay for long periods in that one spot. Pushkin regularly positions himself in a place nearby where he likes to sit, back hunched, under an overhang of delicate but abundant ornamental grasses –

and there he will crouch peering out at the birds, for twenty minutes on end, not quite as invisibly as he would like to think I suspect. Fannie, however, is - or can be - the problem. Much of the time if Michael or I are out in the garden she will sit near one or other of us, on or close to the bench, or stand quietly chewing grass in the field that borders the kitchen window; but if we are not out in the garden, she is unpredictable. Whenever traffic can be heard approaching, especially something large and rattly like a tractor, or lorry, Pushkin invariably runs inside in fright. Fannie, too, can panic, but she is not pathologically frightened of the road as is Pushkin.

On the morning in question, Titus and Pushkin have adopted their regular positions and Fannie is nowhere in sight, but I am presuming she is round the back in the field, when suddenly we all hear a car approaching fast down the lane. Shortly after this, I hear a scratching at the foot of our gate and I see Pushkin and Titus both going towards it. The car is getting ever closer and suddenly Fannie leaps up on to the top of the gate, having been scrabbling around at the bottom. She then hesitates and turns to drop down again on the roadside of the gate as the car is upon us. I lunge at her back and grabbing a handful of her fur pull her inside. As I do this, I register, distantly, that both of us are squawking! Michael sees the tail end of this chain of events from his study window and registers my panic as I come in clutching Fannie in my arms. He shakes his head ruefully and shrugs.

In early September, Jean and Steve come to visit us in the course of their stay in the Yorkshire Dales. They have chosen a glorious sunny day with a strong breeze to come over, and we go for a walk with their gentle collie, Meg. She is the most unpredatory of dogs it is possible to imagine, and they amuse me with their tales of how all animals recognise this softness in Meg. Sheep and cattle in particular will gather round her in a mildly threatening way, knowing that they are completely safe to behave thus. Meg avoids all eye contact with any other animal lest it should arouse a confrontation of any kind. Jean and Steve talk of their two cats, Portia and Nerissa (now there are two superb names to conjure with, given to them by their daughter Tamara while still high from a production of *The Merchant of Venice*), who are a pair of white British Shorthair siblings and who, as kittens, had been stepfathered by another collie – Meg's predecessor, who had become so close to them that he used to carry them around in his mouth and generally take complete care of them. As a result they would both catch live mice for Meg, as they had for her predecessor, and leave them as presents for her in her bed, which completely appalled her and from whom she had to be rescued.

∽

Our perception of the weather in Cumbria since we have been here is that it has been pretty damned wet, while thankfully warm, with the odd spell of glorious summer sun, although from the beginning of July until now, early September, it has rained fairly solidly. However this morning, 4 September, Michael meets local farmer Alan in the village, who bemoans the lack of rain in May and says that they have been trying to catch up ever since. Alan looks across at Michael and solemnly intones:

> Dry April,
> Drop in May,
> To fill the barns
> With corn and hay.

Unfortunately, that drop in May just did not happen this year.

In the south of England many friends have been complaining of the nearly unbearable humidity, but up here in the Lakes it has been fresher and altogether more agreeable, although as wet as any summer I can remember. September began quite as wet as its predecessor, but today dawned as perfect as any summer's day could, cloudless and calm and smelling simply wonderful, and this followed three other days just like this. The nights now have a distinct autumn tang, and on these clear cloudless days even as early as 4.30 in the afternoon the temperature drops enough for me to sneak the heating on for just a quick boost, when Michael isn't looking – for every penny counts in our dire straits with the unsold Moon Cottage.

Another unexpected expense is the wild bird food. There are so many of them and they eat so much! There are an enormous number of tits, far higher than in the South, mainly of the great and blue variety, though with the odd coal tit and, more unusually, long-tailed tits showing up for good measure. It is these very tits that Richard, our neighbour from the Vicarage, refers to as 'fodder' for other predatory birds and mammals. These birds are certainly of a suicidal nature as they constantly fly into the windows of the conservatory, even though there are frames and transfers (of flying birds, ironically) on the panes of glass, intended to warn them off. Often they recover from these head-on collisions, but from time to time we find a dead tit amid the flowers under the window. No other birds have quite this tendency, it appears.

On the feeder on the windowsill outside my study window, in which I keep pine nut kernels, I am visited by a non-stop stream of juvenile chaffinches, with the chests of the males among them just beginning to 'pink' up. At other times, when it is quieter and the tits and chaffinches are away, I will be visited by one or two juvenile goldfinches whose very smart bright yellow and black-and-white tails are somewhat belied by the almost scruffy brown stripy backs and dowdy brown faces, missing the spectacular red and white that their parents sport on their heads. The juveniles seem to relish the pine kernels, whereas their parents prefer the small black niger seeds.

Other regular visitors to the pine kernel feeder are greenfinches and siskins, the females of which have the most beautiful streaked breasts; these two species tend to visit together, but not with any of the other regular visitors. The greenfinches in particular behave quite badly with each other near the feeder. A lot of jockeying for position goes on and sneaky little stabs with the beaks at the back of the bird in front seems *de rigueur*, and they are remarkably noisy with it all. I also get three (surprisingly, as they are strongly territorial) robins, who visit sometimes singly and sometimes as a trio, and one of whom regularly patrols along the roof in a menacing manner and bows up and down a great deal.

I am missing the nuthatches that came regularly throughout July and early August, so the question is where do all the nuthatches go in the late summer? That reminds me too that I have not seen the great spotted woodpeckers for an age either. New visitors to this garden, although Richard says they are regular to his, which is deeply lawned and flowerbedded in a way that ours is not, are blackbirds and song thrushes, and the reason for their incursion into our garden is in order to raid the mass of fleshy red berries that have formed in the last few weeks and are clearly at their peak of ripeness on the deeply poisonous yew tree which stands proudly outside my study window.

Three or four days ago I was aware of one blackbird perching 'shotgun' on the tree, squawking and screeching and carrying on as only blackbirds can, trying to ward off all comers, although the effect of this was to encourage even more birds to come to the tree as far as I can see, as today there were no fewer than four blackbirds and two thrushes. What I do not understand is how the blackbirds and thrushes are able to eat these berries in such huge quantities and suffer no ill effects. I presume they do not digest the poisonous seed, but only its fleshy surround, and that the seed simply passes straight through their gut in a propagating sort of way, and that wherever it lands, if the soil is right there is a good chance that a new yew will grow there. Although this yew stands at around thirty feet high, which is about the same height as the pitch of our roof, it is completely dwarfed by the seven massive Scots pines towering over it at a daunting ninety feet. I love those pines, and there being seven in number I am inclined to name them Bashful, Doc, Dopey, Grumpy, Happy, Sleepy and Sneezy, but dwarves, of course, is what they're not.

CHAPTER 21

Michael and I drive down together to Moon Cottage and, once there, we inevitably talk with a charged intensity about why it hasn't sold.

'I'm sure it's because we haven't said goodbye to it properly, in some way. I know we have to bid our farewells in a sensitive way. Michael, do you remember Stephen saying to me that Moon Cottage will choose who lives in it? I believe he has a special feel for these things.'

'I don't disagree. We left without having sold it and we knew we were going to keep coming back, so it was difficult to say a formal farewell, but how do you suggest we do it?'

'Each of us has to do it in our own way. You do it alone when you want to and how you want to, and so will I.' As I say this, I feel a shaft of pain at the memory of how Michael and Johnny must have felt when they said goodbye to Septi that morning before the vet came for the last time, and this solitary act of taking one's leave of this cottage is, I now realise, a terribly important ritual that we have not hitherto properly observed. We need to ask the absolution of Moon Cottage for leaving it and also to thank it for protecting us and loving us and giving us so much happiness for so long.

There is a lot going on and I never do see how Michael says his goodbye, but I know as night follows day that he does do it in some way of his own and, as I write this, my eyes fill with tears because we sometimes are so insensitive to the glaringly obvious – *of course* we have to make this act of contrition.

I remain in Moon Cottage after Michael returns north again as I have things to do in London, and I too know that I must take my proper leave of the cottage.

On my last morning, I prepare for it for a long time with a strange sense of reluctance and then finally go out into the garden and walk round and round it. I stop in front of Septi's grave for a long moment and say my final adieu to his spirit with the hope that as he is now physically only a skeleton, leaving his bones there is no disrespect to him. I then visit Otto's grave and talk to her for a long time – she, the quintessence of life and youth and freedom who, like so many young cats, under the conviction of invincibility flew across the road into a car and never survived; Otto, the mother of my adored Titus and Fannie, who themselves were never allowed to say their farewell to their birthplace.

'Goodbye, little elf. Fare you well, forgive me for leaving you and taking your two girls with me.'

I enter the cottage and lean against the dear thick walls that have stood there for over 450 years – I enter every room and in some way acknowledge the wattle and daub of it all. I go downstairs and reach up to touch the dark oak beams, first in the dining room and then in the sitting room. I put my fingers in the carvings round the huge antique fireplace and I make my act of emotional and verbal supplication to the cottage, and all that it is and all that it has been and all that it will be; to the many people who have made up its past and to the many people who are yet to live here – I hope so much that they will be as happy as we have been here.

Shortly after this, something happens that makes me feel my contrition has been acknowledged. I am bending over the lavatory bowl involved in a vigorous cleaning exercise, with potential vendors in mind, when I suddenly become aware, really strongly, of scented pipe smoke. As I inhale the fragrance of it, I stand up and remember the 'man who smokes a pipe on the landing' in Shirley's house. She and John always used to laugh at it; he was a benign 'visitor' whom they smelt, but who never physically manifested himself. I am ashamed to say I feel a brief frisson of apprehension as I stand up, still facing the wall.

'Please God, let me not see him. I love him being here, but I just don't want to lay eyes on him.'

With a supreme effort I turn my head around. There is nothing behind me. I walk slowly through the cottage and know that I must go upstairs. I ascend the steep staircase and, although fearful at first, as I climb I am uplifted by an extraordinary sense of well-being and my heart feels lightened. I go into all the bedrooms and I feel sheer happiness. Sunlight is streaming in through the bedroom windows and I notice, with a complete lack of concern, that the windowpanes could do with a clean.

'Ah well, next time, little cottage, next time,' I murmur, and this time, as I get into my car and drive away from the cottage towards the M40 and the northwest, I know that I am properly being allowed to drive to my new home and that I leave behind me Moon Cottage, intact and loved, holding safe all its memories. The cottage has at last said its farewell to us.

I get back to The Old Coach House to find that their ladyships are making much of what is possibly their last oestrus of the year – but blimey, what a kerfuffle. The house is resounding to both the incessant groans from Titus, who can keep it up for what seems like hours at a low rumbling persistent pitch, and the apparently involuntary but strident wails from Fannie, which are more spasmodic but quite deafening in their force. I confess that it really now is altogether too much and it is not only Pushkin who has a headache, but his human companions also. Both the female cats lie in wait for Pushkin, and in the case of Fannie this is the first time she has persistently presented herself to him; but although he kisses their noses with what seems like genuine affection, he continues to tiptoe round them and find places to rest where they will leave him in peace. Our sleep and the sleep of our guests is now regularly being interrupted. Indeed, last night it was so tremendous that I finally resorted to shutting Fannie, Titus and Pushkin in our bathroom, having added a cat litter tray and water. Finally I relented and got up and let Pushkin out, leaving the girls in where they stayed quiet until morning.

Fannie's calling is more ardent than I ever remember it. It usually starts at 1 a.m. and recurs in bursts throughout the hours of darkness, sometimes at the bottom of the stairwell leading up to our open-plan bedroom (oh for a door to just be able to shut her the other side), and sometimes at the bottom of the other stairwell leading up to the guest wing and my study (so when friends are staying overnight, I lie in bed listening to the distant sounds, rigid with guilt). I presume these positions are chosen for their acoustic virility. Michael swears that these strange guttural noises Fannie emits she is completely unable to control – it is true that if you look at her face and her body language when she is doing it, she appears to be quite unaware of it. The sound seems to come from deep within her and emerges as a harsh strident bass cry. It is quite different in tone from the plaintive high cry when she has been shut out and wants to come in, which becomes even shriller if it is raining. This call is primeval and dark and compelling, and why no neighbouring cats come to call can only be because, as everyone in the village assures me, there are no full toms around.

Pushkin is beginning to have a very hang-cat look about him as a result of Fannie's remorseless pursuit of him. She lies in wait for him at every opportunity and calls to him; she rolls on the floor in front of him and in every possible way tries to encourage him. This morning as I am putting down dried food for them I see him very mildly (almost experimentally?) grab Titus, who is busy eating and doing no one any harm, by the scruff of her neck; she immediately lets out a squawk of protest and drops the food in her mouth and strides off in high dudgeon, waving her tail crossly.

'Oh Pushkin, I despair of you. Wrong cat, wrong moment, wrong everything!' He looks up at me and then down again and eats another couple of mouthfuls of dried chicken. The expression on his face remains enigmatic.

'Michael, I am going to have to take them all to the vet. It's simply not fair on them all, this constant unending frustration. The girls are horny as hell and Pushkin is being harassed out of his existence and no one is gaining from this.'

'Hold your horses a moment, Mo. I'm going to talk to Anne at the post office, she'll know if there's anyone around. You know we would both love Fannie to have kittens.'

I duly hold my horses for this day at least and Michael returns later on to tell me that although there are definitely no full tomcats in the village, there is a farm some distance away with the usual assortment of farm cats – which is likely to include at least one tom. The farm is in a village called Lupton and is owned by Alan and Margaret.

'Michael, you can't just ring them up and say "Oi, do you have a stud, please?"'

''Course I can,' he winks as he always does when he's on a roll, and I catch myself apprehensively running my hands through my hair. 'Anyway, there's nothing to stop you doing it if you prefer.'

'I'm doing no such thing.'

'In that case, there's nothing for it, I'll do it. It's now or never.'

'Oh Michael, we have to be so careful. He must be healthy and mustn't have any hateful diseases like feline leukaemia or one of those.'

'The important thing to establish at this stage is whether they have a tom at all, so let's cross that hurdle first.'

He walks across the room and picks up the phone and presses the buttons. I hear only his side of the conversation.

'Yes, that's right. I'm looking for a full tom. Oh good. How old is he. Ah . . . I see. Just a few weeks. No, that wouldn't do the trick. Yes, quite.'

I move across the room and, after more murmurings, I hear Michael begin to make goodbye noises laced with sentiments of gratitude. He pulls a face as he puts the phone down.

'They were really nice and he wanted to be as helpful as possible, but no can do. Not an adult full tom to be had, so now it's back to Plan B then.'

'What's Plan B?'

'The vet and neutering.'

This next night, for the first night in ages, Fannie hardly calls at all, so at last her terrible torture of frustration is at an end.

This morning I received a rather moving letter from Marion Elliott, a reader of both my previous books. She had numerous cats, most of whom adopted her – in fact, all of whom did. Some of these cats were on the wild side, and some had wonderful protective natures and herded their fellow cats to safety – as Septi tried, but gave up, with the wayward Otto. However, Marion says of the death of Cosmic, her beloved and beautiful grey and white kitten with a loving nature who developed feline leukaemia:

> I have never been affected by the death of a cat so much. How my husband drove to the vet's with tears dripping down his face I will never know. We missed Cosmic so much that both Paul and I thought we 'saw' her several times after her death.

This happens. This happened to me and to Michael following the death of Otto. It might have happened to Michael after the death of Septi; certainly the kittens kept jumping around from corners and behaving most strangely immediately after he died, quite as if his spirit was in the cottage and coming to them in some way. And very soon after this, another reader of my books, Doreen Jackson, writes to me of one of her cats from long ago, called Timmy:

> Timmy was a bit of a stop-out at night and wouldn't come in however much we tried, but he

knew if he stretched up and lifted the knocker with his paw and let it fall back hard enough my parents or I would get out of bed and go downstairs to let him in. No one taught him to do it, so it proves that cats use their brains.

CHAPTER 22

Peter Warner, the gifted artist who illustrates these books and who understands so well the idiosyncrasies of our three cats over the time he has worked with them, pays us his first visit to our Cumbrian eyrie. He is surprised to discover how ascendant Titus now is, manifesting full matriarchy within the pecking order of the cats, as the last time he met her she was about to have her leg operation and was in pain and unsteady, which must in turn have contributed to her lack of self-esteem. Fannie, at that time and indeed since the birth of all three kittens, had been the undisputed pack leader. These shifts of power are inscrutable and subtle, but the end results are very clear. I fear for Fannie, who within the new social structure seems to be unsure of how much she may come to me.

Titus spends much of the day on the chair behind me in my study and at regular intervals climbs on to my knee as I type. She is also newly proficient at leaping from a standing start near the door right up on to the desk, often crashing down on to the computer keyboard, a form of invasive behaviour she has learnt from Pushkin and something she could never have done preop. Fannie, who spent almost all day in my study/bedroom in the Moon Cottage days and who in the early weeks at our new house also spent much of the day in my study, will now visit me as little as twice a day. If during these visits Titus is at all assertive as Fannie is considering jumping up on to my lap, Fannie backs right off and immediately leaves the room. She spends much of the time on the bed in the next-door spare room or in an armchair in the conservatory. I feel a pang of guilt towards the other two cats as I recognise the sharp intensity of my own sense of loss within Fannie's affections for me, but equally I remain unsure whether her aloofness is her own uncertainty of what she 'may' do rather than a cooling-off.

For the record, as a rule Pushkin visits my study once a day, usually late in the afternoon, exactly as he did at Moon Cottage, so no change there. He too leaps up on to the desk from the doorway, but he is less clumsy than Titus, so he rarely scatters things around. His foible is that if his visit coincides with my absence from the study he will elegantly sprawl out across the keyboard; but in the course of turning round several times to make sure he finds the warmest and most comfortable position a keyboard can offer, he regularly reprogrammes my computer, and I have learned the hard way to always refuse changes to my 'normal dot'!

I am in awe at the care that Peter Warner takes to make his fluid sketches of the cats. He is able to capture on paper the essence of cat in the most remarkable way. He is astonishingly self-disciplined and will never allow me to gather up and corral the cats in any way to make it easier for him to draw them. He always sketches them where they choose to lie and I have only ever heard him curse under his breath once, when yet again they decide that being stared at with quite this intensity is frankly just too much and they have suddenly thought of a darker, more private place to lie; or, more often than not, the thought of a quick snack crosses their minds, and they shake, turn, stretch and hop down for a quick 'pit-stop'. I conclude

that cats like to watch, but do not like the process to be reversed.

One night, after work for that day has stopped, Peter enraptures me with an account of a cat of his called Pelé. Peter, being the all-rounder that he is, can number among his accomplishments the art of music-making, as well as that of writer and artist. Peter is a jazzman as much as he is a classicist, and many of his cats have been named after jazz musicians. His cat Django (Reinhardt) stood in as a model when he was illustrating the first book* and he needed an older feline statesman to represent Michael's ancient cat, Septi. Django died just days after the book was published, having posed for numerous press photos, and even his first (and last) television appearance around the time of the publication of that book.

So this tale from Peter starts with a cat called Bix (Beiderbecke). Well, actually it really starts with a Great Dane called Nora, who has been used, unscrupulously for five years, as a breeding machine. The rescue is complex and involves Nora disappearing into the large garden where she hides in the middle of a patch of stinging nettles. Here she remains resisting all entreaties to come out. Finally, she is tempted out by a bowl of milk a few days later, and persuaded to come into the house. Peter's household at this time consists of Bunny (Berigan), a tabby Shorthair, Benny (Goodman), a black Shorthair, Bix (Beiderbecke), a seal point Siamese, and now Nora, a black Great Dane. Bix becomes pregnant and gives birth

---

* *The Cats of Moon Cottage* by Marilyn Edwards (Hodder & Stoughton, 2003).

to a litter of three kittens. She has two Siamese kittens, and a totally black kitten with similarly foreign type. This last kitten is apparently born dead. Well, this is what Peter thinks at the time, and Bix rejects it immediately as is often the way of cats when they know one of their litter is ailing or already dead. So the kitten is left in a kitchen cupboard, where it is found, still warm, by a friend, Martha. They try hot and cold water on its heart, and massage it, and in a magical moment it shows signs of life and squeaks. Nora, the Great Dane, hears this and takes the 'dead' kitten and licks it and licks it. As he is telling me the tale, Peter adds:

> It was extraordinary to watch it. She believed in that kitten and its possibility of life. She licked it back into being. And slowly, slowly, he recovered, for he it was. I named him Pelé for his speed and turning ability, thus breaking the jazz name mould, but appropriate to his new canine identity. His mother never did accept him or feed him and we had to feed him with a dropper. As the kitten grew up, he would often play right inside

Nora's mouth, and submit to bathtime by tongue.
There was an astonishing trust and bond between
them. She would even shut her mouth with him
inside, but he remained calm and unharmed.

Pelé grows up to be a handsome black cat, and walks
often with Peter, Nora and Lorraine (who was the one
who made Peter rescue Nora) to a local pub, and he
learns to hide inside Peter's coat when crossing the road,
and while in the pub.

When Pelé is about six years old, Peter has been on a
day trip to see his father in Burgess Hill, some thirty
miles distant from his own house. He returns that night

to find that Pelé is missing. Two days later, his father phones him to say:

'Peter, I could swear that today I saw the spitting image of Pelé just across the road from me. But just at that moment a lorry drove past and after it had gone there was no sign of any cat.'

Peter becomes increasingly concerned about his little black cat and alerts all his neighbours to keep their eyes open for him. Four days after Peter's trip to Burgess Hill, Pelé turns up on the doorstep, dusty, dirty and hungry. Having eaten and drunk, he sleeps for hours and hours.

'So, unbelievable though it may sound,' Peter continues the tale, 'I believe that Pelé took it into his head to come and find me in Burgess Hill. He was altogether a remarkable cat – he used to play with a pen when you were writing, and it could really be quite difficult to continue. But the extraordinary thing was that he never, ever interfered with pencil or a brush. He would just watch the business end of it with absolute concentration.' As he says this, Peter does a wonderful imitation of Pelé, shaking his head from side to side in the most catlike manner. As I laugh I wonder to myself if Peter is himself a reincarnated cat. He *can* draw cats as no other, and I see now that he moves as a cat does too!

Peter then adds sadly:

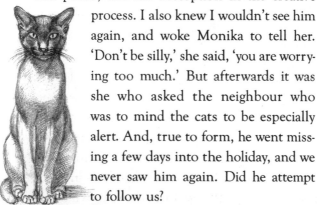

That summer I went on holiday to Somerset. The night before leaving, Pelé came on to the bed as I read, and fixed me with that all knowing and infinite gaze cats have, and in that moment I knew he was William Blake. I've no idea where that thought came from, just an absolute conviction. It explained Pelé's distinction between pen and pencil, and his absorption in the creative process. I also knew I wouldn't see him again, and woke Monika to tell her. 'Don't be silly,' she said, 'you are worrying too much.' But afterwards it was she who asked the neighbour who was to mind the cats to be especially alert. And, true to form, he went missing a few days into the holiday, and we never saw him again. Did he attempt to follow us?

Shortly after Peter returns to the South, Halloween draws ever closer and I am more aware of this day than I ever normally would be because it is the first anniversary of the death of my friend and once literary agent Giles Gordon, and I am filled with a deep sense of my own loss for this remarkable man. I find that I am thinking a lot about his family and all those who love him. In spite of my awareness of this, however, I am caught completely off guard when, up to my ears in grouting some tiles around the shower, I hear the doorbell ring. I race downstairs complete with spatula and a fist-full of drying grout to discover two attractive girls in their early teens dressed respectively as an angel and a devil. I open the door, flapping my encumbered hands feebly, and am afterwards told by the she-devil that I say:

'Oh shit!' which I learn is the first time she has been greeted in quite this welcoming way. I continue, marginally more graciously:

'Sorry, sorry, what I mean is, I'm up to my ears in

grouting and it's drying really fast and I know that Michael took all my change and I don't have any sweets in the house, oh dear, oh dear. Forgive me.'

Both girls laugh, indeed in a forgiving way, and the she-devil says: 'Don't worry, it's all right. It's just trick or treat night.' I swallow hard and smile back at them both, really gratefully. Trick or treat night in the Dales used to get quite 'heavy', as it did around Moon Cottage, with serious reprisals if no treat was forthcoming.

Two days later I receive a phone call from Hilary, asking me if I have a cat carrier. (Hilary, whom I mentioned earlier in the context of Heathcliff and Toby, made us feel very welcome early on by inviting us to a riotous birthday party, and who, I have been told by several people, is one of the most significant bonding elements within the village because loving people with a passion, she adores any excuse for getting everyone together to celebrate and raise a glass.) I say yes, of course, would she like to borrow it? And she then says:

'A small black kitten has been found and we don't know who owns him and he needs some veterinary treatment and I'm really not sure that I can keep him.'

My mind races as she says all this, as I'm not sure whether she wants to find him a home, and I know that another small tom into the mix of cats within the confines of The Old Coach House is not going to be the answer for my venerable crew of felines. She continues:

'He has lice and also he seems to be incontinent.' As she adds this, I feel my enthusiasm for this tiny creature of the night waning and I feel completely guilt-ridden. But at this point she adds, philosophically:

'I know it's hopeless and I'll end up keeping him anyway, because we have already given him a name. He is black and shiny, exactly like a little olive, so he is called Oliver, but he's already become Ollie. I'll pop up now and get your cage.' And shortly afterwards she lands on the doorstep and I duly hand over the cage, wishing her all luck.

Michael and I have to go away and have coerced Elspeth and Clive to stay in our house with the small request that could they just look after the little menagerie for us? As the time arrives, however, I leave the house feeling completely guilt-ridden. On the night before our departure, Fannie is so frantic with her writhing and calling on our bed that I hold her by the neck and bring Pushkin to her. She makes the pre-nuptial screaming sound that is peculiar to queens in oestrus, but exceptionally loudly at which point Titus comes clumping up the stairs and runs into the room. Pushkin, who jumps down on to the floor the second I let him go, is sitting the other side of the room. He and I look at each other with probably identical expressions of surprise on our faces. Fannie is still making her screaming noises even though I am no longer holding her and nor have been for some time. At this point Titus jumps up on to the bed, walks purposefully towards Fannie, and hits her across her face with her left paw, hard enough for a 'thwack' sound to be audible to the human ear. Fannie immediately falls silent and then turns over on her back into the full submissive position with her front paws bowed over and her head tipped towards her sister. Titus stays on the bed, crouched, and watches her but makes no further move. On reflection, it is almost as if Titus was trying to shut her up rather than be aggressive, but I'm simply not sure. But I do know now that I must have Fannie and Titus neutered. This is simply not fair to either of them, as it seems to me that they may even be suffering to some extent, added to which it is now becoming unending and enough is definitely enough.

The following day, before I can change my mind, I phone up the surgery and make an appointment for Gerard to neuter the two girls and castrate Pushkin. The appointment is made for December, well after we return from France.

Elspeth and Clive arrive at The Old Coach House late on the night of the day we have already left, so I am unable to speak to Elspeth until the following day. When we do catch up with each other on the phone, she is very relaxed and forgiving, which is far more than I deserve.

'They are being very good and Titus is schmoozing up to Clive. She has been sitting on his knee. But today Fannie climbed on my shoulders and stayed up there and I was able to walk around with her, and she regularly comes across and talks to me. Pushkin just seems to wander about and he comes in and out of the rooms where we are sitting, but mainly he does his own thing. Fannie is being a bit frantic though!'

I am enormously reassured that the cats are OK and also that Elspeth is being so understanding about Fannie. But I am ashamed for my pang of envy that Fannie is responding so positively to Elspeth, who is a real cat person, and who I knew would win her over, but I so miss the closeness I had always had with her in the past, and even at this distance wonder how I might recapture it. But I do know how lucky we are to have such wonderful friends who are prepared to come and look after the cats in this way.

CHAPTER 23

We return home to find The Old Coach House and its cats in apple pie order. As I follow Michael into the house, having heard his calls to all the cats while I have been unpacking the car, I echo the reparation that he has already performed. The rite I speak of is that of attempting to stroke the cats, while each of them exacts their own need to respond with complete avoidance of any human contact. Fannie winds herself between the legs of the piano stool, holding her tail erect and shivering, and then tentatively greets me first fondly by a small forward advance, and then distantly, by jumping up on to the top of the piano, which is just inside the front door, in order to take stock of all that is going on, as is always her way when we return from a trip involving a number of nights' absences. I bend down to stroke Titus and she shuns every kind of caress with overt disdain. She actively shakes off the touch of a stroking hand with a wriggle and a shimmy and a tail waving crossly from side to side. This is her way of dealing with our betrayal. And Pushkin is nowhere to be seen, which is emphatically his way at all times regardless of whether we have been away for days or merely hours. As we finish hauling in our suitcases and other artefacts from the car, Pushkin finally emerges, yawning, and head butts us each in turn. At least this time he seems to know who we are. Now Titus, too, is prepared to speak, and in her manner greets us with an open mouth and a rusty-sounding miaow.

We do the chores we need to and then start to get ready for bed. The cats perform their time-honoured ritual of all coming up to witness the-entering-of-the-bed-routine. And each must be stroked in turn. (On reflection, that latter is our ritual, my ritual even, rather than theirs!) Pushkin usually sits on the stairs and watches, apart from the other two, while Fannie and Titus both lie on the bed until all the lights are put out, when they thumpily jump down and go to their sleeping places elsewhere in the house.

The following day is what the gently spoken Irish captain of our plane had announced as being a 'soft' one – that is, faintly misty but with a low autumnal sun breaking through it, sending long shafts of gold to the far edges of all the fields and making the drops of water on the long grasses and the leaves in the hedgerows sparkle. I bounce down to the kitchen to start the coffee percolating and as I look out of the kitchen window I see an amazing sight. Cows, thirteen large Friesians cows (except, under scrutiny, they turn out to be three-quarter grown heifers who, from time to time and with no apparent provocation other than for the sheer hell of it, stop their gentle rhythmic grazing and instead boisterously mount each other), are gently pottering around the three interlinked fields that come right up to our kitchen window, and that in the summer months serve as a small campsite and separate us from the thick woodland behind that climbs up to the top of the crags.

I love having those beautiful beasts close to me. They exude a calm and gentleness behind their great size that is profoundly comforting, and the sweet clean breath of cattle is one of my favourite smells in the whole world. (It is strange, and to me most sad, that the synonyms for bovine in most thesauruses are untrue negatives

such as dense, dozy, dull, slow, sluggish, stolid, stupid, thick – they are not these things.)

I rush back up to our bathroom whose back window overlooks the field, with a higher and therefore longer view, and I find Fannie reared up on top of the towel rail with her back legs on the towels and her front feet up on the windowsill, her whiskers thrust forward, quivering. As I stand next to her she turns to look at me with her eyes large in fear. She jumps down. She jumps up again, laboriously clambering up on to the side of the bath, and from there higher still on to the washbasin, then up to the towel rail, and so on, to the windowsill. She presses her nose to the window and makes a low growling noise. As we both watch through the window, one of the nearest heifers moves a couple of yards further forward to reach a new clump of grass and Fannie gasps in fright and jumps straight down on to the floor, groaning slightly as the breath is knocked out of her as she hits the deck and races off to look through other windows. For the next half-hour or so Fannie intermittently stares out of every window in the house. Sheep routinely surround us, although not usually in the field that now contains the heifers, and even when we first moved here I never remember the cats responding to the sheep in this way. They did watch them, slightly warily, but not with the fear that the heifers are engendering now. The size of these beasts is of course considerably greater, and yet for the moment Fannie has only seen them through a window, which is not the same as being a tiny cat at the hoof of a Friesian cow when the differential in size would be truly awesome.

As soon as I am able I phone up Elspeth and establish that she and Clive were perfectly happy during their stay.

'Tell me, tell me, though – when did the cows first come in?'

'What cows? We never saw any cows.'

I explain, and Elspeth reckons that they must have been put into the field on the Monday that we got back, so in fact when I saw Fannie freaking out in the bathroom, it most probably was the first time she had set eyes on them.

~

We wake up this morning and there has been the first ground frost of the autumn, not severe, but it feels astonishingly chilly in our unheated bedroom with its three windows. Following a grisly day yesterday in which both Michael and I had sunk into the pits of despair about Moon Cottage and its lack of sale, I instinctively know this one will not be so shabby. We now have the heating on for a burst of an hour in the morning, which brings the house up to a bearable temperature. Michael is sounding cheery and bouncy and his normal noisy self, and I hear him drive off to Kirkby Lonsdale for the Saturday newspapers, and shortly after he returns he shouts up to the bathroom that he has done a fry-up, bless him. I come running down, and not only is there beautiful bacon and egg, there is piping-hot coffee and hot toast and marmalade. So wonderful, what indulgence! As we sit down together and look out through those windows across the valley, and to the hills and over to Ingleborough on the other side, I have never seen it all look more beautiful, on any day, than it does today and I feel tears come to my eyes.

'I know exactly what you are thinking and so am I,' Michael says as he picks up my hand. 'We cannot leave here, we mustn't leave here. *We mustn't!*'

'Yup, that's it in one,' I whisper back squeezing his hand. He hits the table with the heel of his free hand more triumphantly than despairingly I choose to think.

I clear up the late breakfast things and walk into the kitchen with my arms full of crocks, and as my eye is drawn towards the light I realise that I am looking through a glass dimly as the large plate glass kitchen window is streaked with a curious opaque film. I have to conclude that this is the legacy of the teenage giants in our field outside who have been spending a few idle moments licking the window in that way that they do, and artistically cross-hatching it with blades of grass. I go outside and clean the window, knowing full well that in a few minutes, or possibly a few hours, it will no doubt be opaque again, but I can live with that!

Tonight we go off to the village hall where we, along

with all other villagers, have been invited to join in the French Night, the rules for admission being that you must wear something recognisably French, you must speak with a French accent, and you must take one course, either a starter, main or pudding (and which must also be French, *naturellement*), enough to feed the number of you attending. Michael and I both don French berets, which we wear normally anyway, so this is a bit of a cop-out. For the food, I rather unimaginatively open a tin of two dozen snails, the French edible kind of course. When we arrive, with the mandatory French stick apiece clamped under our arms and clutching a couple of bottles of Bordeaux, we rather embarrassingly find that everyone else is already seated, that the hall is full of folk, that there is a French stick mountain, and that loads of other people have taken snails too – so in the end we find ourselves eating snails and more snails, and also someone else's frogs legs, which have in fact been cooked to perfection.

We find a couple of free seats at a table near us and sit down to find that we are on the same table as Hilary and her husband, Phil, so I hungrily ask for news of

what is happening with the 'Halloween' kitten. The last report I had from a mutual friend was that he was still incontinently not performing in his cat litter tray, and I am well aware that Hilary is really concerned about how long she will be able to put up with that state of affairs.

'Marilyn, he is just the most gorgeous cat in the world. He is still tiny and adorable and there is no way I would give him up now. Please promise me you will come down and see him as soon as you can.'

The evening becomes more animated as large quantities of French wine are consumed, and in between the last two courses various couples are asked to change tables. Michael and I nominate ourselves, as we are the new kids on the block, and we move across to a neighbouring table. Shortly after we have joined our new table we are all issued with a quiz sheet consisting of questions to do with people, subjects and things French, and we make a reasonable fist of our collective answers – although we only come third or fourth in the final score. The couple who are filling in our quiz sheet are called Jeff and Karen. In a lull in the proceedings, someone mentions cats and I gaily shout across the table at Jeff and Karen:

'Do you have a cat?' Karen looks across the table at me and her face twists sadly. She replies:

'We did until two weeks ago.' I feel terrible and ask them what happened. Tinkerbell, their beautiful long-bodied, long-haired black and white cat, who was a real character (and all the people on our table enthusiastically vouch for what a sweetie he was), had gone missing one very windy day when Jeff was working on the village hall. When Jeff got home at lunchtime and found that Tinks was nowhere to be seen, he already knew something was amiss because Tinks never missed coming back to greet him at lunch time; so, with a heavy heart, that afternoon he went off hunting for him.

Eventually he found him in an unused sewage drainpipe lying alongside the wall of a field. He had been wounded, probably by a vehicle, and his instinct must have led him to crawl inside the pipe so that he might die undisturbed. By the time Jeff found him, rigor mortis had set in.

'I think that the wind was responsible. He must've been so deafened by the noise that he simply failed to hear a vehicle approaching him.'

Even though I have several times experienced the pain and sense of loss that the death of a beloved animal causes you, it is supremely hard to find any words that might give proper comfort to a family so recently bereaved, and I think I probably resort to all clichés known to man and woman, and probably the only cliché I consciously avoid is the unhelpful one of 'life must go on'.

As it turns out, this day does end less buoyantly than it began because when we finally return home after the ten yards' walk from the village hall to The Old Coach House at the end of this splendid French Evening, our boiler, which heats not just the radiators but is also the only source of hot water, is flashing its emergency 'lock-out' light, indicating it is no longer functioning; although we have learnt to live without heating, living without hot water is, for me, just too awful to bear. The following morning we ask our serenely accommodating neighbour, Annabel, who rescues us uncomplainingly from all our domestic plights, who might help us this time and when, yet again, she flicks through her little black book to give Michael the appropriate telephone number, Michael realises happily that the Jeff whose number she is proffering is the very same Jeff who was our table companion on the previous evening.

He comes, even though it is Sunday, like a knight in shining armour and by Monday, with the appropriate spare part in his hand, Jeff has got our boiler in full working order again. After he has finished working on the boiler I urge him to talk some more about Tinkerbell, but not without experiencing a little guilt as I sense the pain I am stirring up. As he gently talks about their much-loved cat, I slowly grasp, with over-whelming sadness, that the beautiful cat who had come calling late at night in the summer when Stephen was with us must have been Tinks and that I had often seen him as I had driven through the village, hunting in the hedges near the dry stone walls at the far end. In fact, his full name was Tinkerbell, although once his masculinity was established he was always known in the family as either Tinks or Bella. (I'm not the only one to sex kittens wrongly!) Tinks was one of a litter of four kittens, two tortie and two black and white, born two and a half years ago to a neighbouring friend of theirs called Catherine. Their oldest daughter, Lesley, worked on Jeff to persuade him that, having vaguely spoken to some vet somewhere, it would not cost more than £15 to give the kitten all the injections it needed and, she continued, he would be great company for her, her brother Neil and, especially, for their much younger sister, Alex. Jeff laughs wryly:

'Load of rubbish of course, it costs far more than her £15, but by then we were hooked and he was part of our family. He was such a patient cat as well as loving, and would let himself be picked up and dragged around like a little doll without complaining. He loved to lie on his back and have his tummy tickled. I had had a cat of my own when I was in primary school, which I had swapped for two dinky toys, so I did know how she felt. But Tinks was a really special cat and the kids chose him themselves out of all the litter. They had the chance to work out which one it was to be as when the kittens were very young we looked after them all for a spell, and Tinks was the one for them. He loved people.'

'I always think,' I offer, 'and many of the cat manuals say this, that cats that have been socialised from a very early age, and handled by a large number of people when they are very young, prove to be the friendliest of cats when they mature.' Jeff nods quietly.

'He had been brought up with a cat litter tray, and for a long time he would never go outside, but always come back inside to use his litter tray. Sometimes at night he would stop out until late. Although he had been neutered he was still interested in the ladies, I reckon, and if I woke up in the night and knew he was still out and went down to let him in, he would shoot past me just as if he had missed the last bus, and race over to the food bowl to eat whatever might still be in it.'

I ask Jeff if they will look for another kitten or cat,

but he delays answering and when I pursue it further, he shrugs in a sad way and says out of respect for Tinks's memory he would rather not just yet. But cats always seem to present themselves when you are least expecting them, and anyway it isn't just down to him of course, but the whole family who are missing him, so they may get one sooner rather than later.

Shortly after this conversation, Karen and Jeff, when out walking with their two girls, Lesley and Alex, call on us to see all the cats and I tease Lesley about her scam on the price of injections, but she reckons it was well worth it. She and Alex between them tell me that shortly before Tinks was killed they had taken him to see Gerard, the vet, because Tinks alone out of the four kittens had been born with a heart murmur, and Gerard always liked to check he was in good health. Tinkerbell's purr was always so consistently loud that Gerard would unfailingly have to put his fingers over Tinkerbell's nose to stop the purring, so he could hear his heartbeat through his stethoscope. Lesley and Alex both say to me sadly that their family has had bad luck with animals as Lesley's horse had to be put down, Neil had problems with his dogs and they had to be rehomed, and now Tinkerbell has died. I try to reassure them that it is not bad luck, and there will bound to be more animals in their lives soon.

Animals often die before what we feel should be their due time, but I do reckon it should never put us off loving another animal again, because that limitless flow of love to be given and received between people and the animals they live with, if they are lucky enough to be able to do this, is truly life enhancing. I know, tetchy thing that I am, that I am better by far with animals in my life than without them, and that is in spite of the love of Michael.

The following week an irresistible desire to go and see young Ollie takes me down to Hilary's house. (I have always suffered badly from kitten-lust, but truth to tell I also want my cat carrier back as I feel slightly uneasy without it in case of emergency.) Sure enough, this fluff-bundle of what seems to me pure black heaven is flying round Hilary's hall, batting a wine cork about with his two front feet, alternately equal to the skill of that shown only by the greatest of the ball masters.

This is definitely a Georgie or a Becks if ever I saw one. (Could it even be a reincarnation of Peter's Pelé I wonder to myself?) Hilary tells me that Catherine, her youngest daughter, first wanted to call him Pepper because of the tiny traces of silver hairs in his otherwise immaculate 'pure' black coat, and after that she wanted to call him Charlie because he clearly must have fallen off a witch's broomstick, appearing as he did from nowhere, a completely black cat, on the day after Halloween.

'But anyway, Ollie he is and he is definitely staying.' On gentle enquiry I learn that the adorable black kitten in front of me, who lies on his back and waves his paws in the air and stares up at me with the greenest of green eyes and who the vet reckons is about three months old, has now mastered the use of the litter tray and also goes outside. All the health problems that he had on arrival have sorted themselves out and he is shaping up to be a much-loved and very loving small cat. Ollie, too, has now properly befriended Thomas, Hilary's and Phil's beautiful thick-pelted grey tabby aged seven, and lord of his domain until this moment. Hilary laughs as she says:

'Thomas was so good with him under the circumstances. He hissed a couple of times. He belted him once and then, with only the smallest sigh, he accepted him into his world.' Just as I am about to take my reluctant leave of Ollie, Peter and Catherine both return from school and we talk for a little; and it is then that I discover, to my intense embarrassment, that the she-devil I so inelegantly greeted on All Hallows Eve was none other than young Catherine, accompanied by her close friend, the angel Hayley!

CHAPTER 24

A tiny paragraph appears in the gossip column of the *London Evening Standard* about Moon Cottage being up for sale, but it is so obscure that I cannot believe it will actually generate a sale; but, who knows, perhaps the longed-for miracle will happen. Michael and I have another serious conversation in which he makes me understand exactly how much money we are losing and he warns me that we may yet have to sell up here and move back down to Moon Cottage. We seem unable either to rent or sell and the tension for us both is painful.

We are not sleeping well, and this sleeplessness is

being made even more unremitting for us both by Fannie's strident guttural calling, which she does every two hours right through the night. She seems to trot up and down the corridor that runs from the bottom of our stairs to the sitting room door, pausing at each of the conservatory windows in turn, and then shrieks her lustful cry to the world, but no tom comes a-calling. Sometimes I lie in bed and I hear her voice very distantly and far off, then I realise she must be up in the spare room calling out of that window, and then the cycle starts all over again.

One day I am sitting at my computer and she starts; it is worse at night, but she does call during the daytime too – and for the umpteenth time I go into a website called www.studcat.co.uk. My eye is suddenly caught by a cat stud in Lancashire under the heading of SKYBLUE PINKSIAMESE & ORIENTALS, in which the breeder has used the phrase:

Storm is a much-loved Stud cat, lovely temperament, super blue eyes, but not very typy bodywise. He sires wonderful kittens and is most kind and gentle to his girls, especially maiden queens. Inspection welcome any time.

I am much taken with the compassion in tone for her stud, the honesty of the absence of 'typy', and moved by the thought that gentleness with a first-time queen is a consideration. Lancashire is a big county, but the stud might just be close to the Cumbrian border. There is an email address and so, feeling I have nothing to lose, I nervously send off an exploratory email. Herewith is an extract of the reply:

From:	Marje and Ian
To:	Marilyn
Sent:	Wednesday, 17 November, 18:54
Subject:	Re: Siamese/Oriental Stud and your help please

```
Dear Marilyn
  Yes, I can help...
  My cat Storm is not very well but he
has a son by the name of Skybluepink
Zimmy who is an experienced virgin
woo-er. He is an Oriental Apricot. As
he is an Apricot and belongs to the
```

red family he would go brilliantly with your tortie colourwise. Regarding the rest I cannot say.

Zimmy has very, very, very, very naughty clever kittens, very bright and very beautiful.

I do require that your cat has a blood test, but I can get this done here. Zimmy of course is done and up to date with inoculations. He lives in a heated pen outside my patio window, is a pain in the bum, and is very noisy and very nosy. He has creature comforts, fur beds, heated oil-filled radiator, evening lights and a radio, plus of course passing leaves floating down, birdies in trees and me.

I like to keep the cats about a week. He is free now if you can get her down real soon.

Marjorie

The attached picture in the email shows a slim, elegant apricot-coloured Oriental cat, tall and handsome with a faintly arrogant look to him. He has rings on his tail and faint stripy markings (which when I see him in the flesh I discover are intermingled with superb leopard spots), and he sports the distinctive large pointed ears endemic to the Oriental breed. As I look at the picture repeatedly I find myself feeling mildly apprehensive, because this is like choosing a mate by catalogue, but at the same time I am also much taken with the idea of this striking-looking cat, named after Zimmy the lion, husbanding my little Fannie. I ask Michael what he thinks we should do. He replies simply:

'Well, it's now or never.'

That evening I talk to Marjorie on the phone and find she is reassuring and kind, as well as businesslike. So, without more ado, the following day, a Thursday, finds Michael driving a car with me in the back behind a wire fireguard separating us from the driving area, with Fannie on my knee and the cat carrier next to us heading straight down the M6 towards east Lancashire and Rossendale. It is a bitterly cold, grey November day and Fannie is not at all happy at her enforced journeying, and intermittently wails forlornly and most unlustfully. After two hours we reach our destination and, after talking things through, we finally bid them farewell, leaving Fannie behind us. As we walk away from the house I feel a total rat. I have transported my virgin girl to a strange house a long way from home containing a male stud who has only one thought in his head. While Fannie was in Marjorie's sitting room Zimmy came into the room and immediately came up to the side of the carrier and sniffed repeatedly through the side, and then he walked all round it and yowled, oh how he yowled. Zimmy has a very big voice. Fannie stared at him with large eyes through the bars. It was a totally inscrutable expression she bore on her face.

As Michael gently manoeuvres the car out on to the main road and we head off towards the M62 motorway, large lumps of water hit the windscreen heavily.

'Michael, it's sleeting. We're going to get the first snow of this winter. Yikes!'

'Mmmmn!' he replies, non-committally.

'Whaddya mean "Mmmmn"?' I ask.

'I was just thinking, poor Fannie.'

'Don't do that,' it's now my turn to wail. 'I feel bad enough without you saying stuff like that. Whaddya mean "poor Fannie"?'

'Well I s'pose what I'm trying to say is she'll be very upset for a few hours, and she's now got to go to the vet for that blood test, and then she'll be put out into the shed and it's really cold outside now and she'll be all by herself and she'll miss Titus – I should think she might even miss Pushkin, but . . .' there's a sigh, and then a laugh '. . . but by tomorrow morning I expect she'll have a smile on her face.'

'Oh, typical man!'

'Hey, it was your idea, coming here. You found Zimmy, not me.'

As we drive homewards the sleet falls more heavily, and as we near the high hills of home we see a ring of snow on the peaks. It is very beautiful but deadly cold.

As we walk inside the house, I shudder fretfully. Titus greets me in a rather dull sort of way. She is clearly looking for Fannie. Pushkin is nowhere to be seen.

I go up to my study and wonder how soon it will be acceptable for me to phone Marjorie to find out how things are. As I turn round from my desk to look at the armchair where normally I would expect to see Fannie and Titus together, rolled up in companionably adjacent balls, I am somewhat disconcerted to see Pushkin and Titus together instead, lying next to each other like two large peas in a pod.

'Didn't take you long, boy, did it?' I enquire gently of Pushkin. He just looks dolefully across at me, sighs long-sufferingly, and puts his head back down again.

It is now Thursday evening and Fannie has been with her stud for one whole day and I feel the need to get an update from Marjorie. We speak on the phone but Marjorie also does me a very funny series of emails as if from Fannie, and from these two sources I discover that Fannie has passed her blood test, she is in a pen next to Zimmy, hissing at him at regular intervals, and the plan is that tomorrow, Friday, she will be let out of her inner sanctum and put in the bigger cage with Zimmy.

The following evening Marjorie phones me with a further update and tells me that Fannie is eating well, but that she is continuing to hiss and slash out at Zimmy, who remains stoically unfazed by her hostility. The snow is heavy and the weather very cold, but Marjorie soothes my disquiet by assuring me that Fannie has a hot water bottle under her bedding and that she is next to a warm radiator. She has not let the two cats alone together yet, but only under her supervision, as Fannie is still hissing regularly.

I spend a restless night worrying about her. The following morning I go into email and find this:

From:	Marje and Ian
To:	Marilyn
Sent:	Saturday, 20 November, 10:58
Subject:	HRH Lady Fannie

```
TO WHOM IT MAY CONCERN
   This Royal notice is to confirm that
Fannie (now known as HRH Lady Fannie)
was mated by Skybluepink Zimmy after
```

```
several hundred tries at 10.15 a.m.
this morning. She is now laid out on
the lounger posing for pictures.
  Marje K
```

I email Marje, immediately asking her to congratulate Zimmy and to say what a great boy he has been, but I also tell her that at around that time on Saturday, Titus suddenly miaowed out really loudly for no reason that either of us could determine. Shortly after this I telephone her and inquire how soon I might collect the Lady Fannie, but she tells me firmly that I must leave Fannie with Zimmy for several more days yet to be certain that he has properly fertilised her, and now I find I am becoming, somewhat tardily, fiercely protective of Fannie. That night, the Saturday night, I am wide awake from 2.30 a.m. onwards. The cold spell has lessened its iron grip slightly, but I still worry about how low the temperature is at night. Now, however, I am even more concerned that Zimmy's attentions might become suffocatingly overzealous and am aware that if

Fannie were out in the wild she would have the option of running away, which she cannot do in her little cage. Eventually, in the dull grey light of early morning I creep up to my study and email the long-suffering Marjorie to say that I really would like to come today.

Just as we are about to leave for church the phone rings and it is Marjorie. She is not pleased with me. As tactfully as she can, she tries to dissuade me from coming over and collecting Fannie. She really wants Zimmy and Fannie to have more time together and believes that I am going to mess things up by collecting Fannie too early. I know I am being difficult and groan with embarrassment. After a further agonised conversation I say that I will phone her later in the day. While I am in church I pray for some sign that I can interpret as guidance on what best to do. We return to The Old Coach House and I race up to my computer just in case Marjorie has emailed me while we have been out, and I find an email saying I can collect Fannie.

I prepare to leave The Old Coach House as soon as I have read the email. The weather has now turned very wet and foggy as the cold gives way to a rapidly enveloping warm front. I remember almost nothing about that journey except the fog and the lights and the drippiness of it all and an extraordinarily heightened sense of pleasure and anticipation that I shall be seeing my girl, that she is fit and well, that she will soon be safely back home, and that she may well be a-mother-to-be. Marjorie and Ian welcome me, with an air of mild surprise that I have got there so quickly. We do all the paperwork and then, with all the boring bits sorted, we go to the pen that is housing Zimmy and Fannie, and there they both are lying together on a fur-covered upright chair.

Some few moments after Marjorie and I have entered the pen with the intention of putting Fannie into her carrier, I become aware of Zimmy quietly but deliberately grabbing Fannie by the back of her neck, high up near her ears, and without further ado he mounts her and promptly mates with her. I feel extreme discomfiture at being there and try to move away, but Marjorie persuades me that I should stay and let it be. After a suitable passage of time during which Fannie is able to regain her composure, I go across to her and attempt to place her in the cat carrier, which is standing on a high table.

She resists this at the beginning, but in the end I manage
to reverse her in. Just as I am
closing the wire-fronted door,
Zimmy stands up on his rear legs
to his full height and puts his paw
through the door to touch Fannie.
He then stretches his head right up and touches her
nose with his. As their noses touch she gives him a tiny
lick. Marjorie is really moved by the affection that her
stud boy is showing towards my wayward little queen –
and the whole episode makes me feel I need to take
Fannie away as quickly as possible before we become
hopelessly emotional. Just as we are about to leave,
Marjorie nearly does make me cry by very shyly giving
me a wonderful curly cottony wool blanket for 'Lady

Fannie' to lie on, as a memento of her mating with Zimmy.

As I drive off into the murky grey November day, Fannie, whose cat carrier is strapped on to the front passenger seat with the door facing me, presses her face against the wire grill and mewls long and sadly. I cannot gainsay whether it be for the loss of Zimmy or for the horror of yet another car journey, or simply for the whole bang shoot of it. I talk to her and gently stroke her through the bars and I feel the rough warm pull of her tongue on my fingers as she licks me in greeting. She and I have missed each other and we have a lot to say to each other, whatever else might have been happening.

At our journey's end I unload the car and remove anything that might have the smell of Zimmy on it, lest it disrupt the status quo. Marjorie has suggested I cover all three Coach House cats with a small sprinkling of talcum powder, which I do, the intention being to confuse them all, but the smell of Zimmy on Fannie is clearly very strong and overrides all other scents. Titus, whom I had expected to welcome Fannie as if she were the prodigal daughter, is clearly very ill at ease and behaves most strangely the second that I release Fannie into the house. She stares at Fannie with big eyes and with what looks like hostility or fear showing in them. Fannie quickly sidesteps Titus and rushes into the kitchen where she eats rapidly. As soon as she has taken the first edge off her hunger she runs upstairs to my study. She climbs on the chair. She jumps down again, and runs the length of the house and up into our bedroom.

I find Pushkin in the spare room unaware at this moment that Fannie is back in the house. I put him in the same room together with Fannie to see what, if anything, might happen. He is fascinated by her smell but again, as with Titus, she sidesteps him and trots off, tail up, pursuing her own business and checking, checking, checking, and then I hear her clattering around the food bowls again. While she is distracted with eating, Titus keeps making dives at her rear end to sniff for the story of what has been happening and at one point I see Titus round the back of the sofa pushing her whiskers into Pushkin's ear.

'Michael, I just saw Titus whispering to Pushkin round the back of the sofa!'

'You are really losing it, Marilyn. Call yourself an animal behaviourist. Cats don't talk, OK?'

It looked like whispering to me, whatever anyone says!

That night Marjorie phones me to check that we have got home in one piece and I assure her that all is well and we talk about when I may see the first signs of whether Fannie is pregnant, and also at what point she will have passed the danger of aborting. Marjorie reckons that certainty of a pregnancy will only be ascertained at five weeks from the mating, as by that time Fannie will start to show, or, if there are any problems, she will have naturally aborted by that time. That takes us to early January, and until then I will just have to be very patient. What will be will be.

So slowly, gently, everything subsides into its normal, or near normal rhythm, although that first evening when Fannie tries to lie next to Titus, Titus hisses long and loudly and eventually Fannie gets down. Pushkin, who has taken to lying in that chair, only lies in it now when the other two cats are away, and Fannie is even climbing back up on to the top of her wardrobe, which Titus briefly took over as her domain. In other words, it seems to me that the status quo has reverted to how it was before the recent power struggle when Titus became the ascendant cat.

This weekend my sister Margot, her husband David, and their son Laurence come to stay with us. Laurence's sister, Victoria, is in the last week of her absolutely frantic first term at Cambridge and understandably cannot be distracted from it at any price. It is the very first time any member of my family has come to see the new house since we moved here in April and I am longing for it more than I can say. They arrive more quickly than I had estimated their journey would take them and I am out shopping for food, so when I get back Michael has had the pleasure of showing them the house and I am childishly disappointed, as I had so wanted to see what they thought of it. I think they like it, but I missed whatever first impression it made on them. As I walk in, however, I am confronted by the sight of Margot desperately trying to move Titus off her knee without touching her fur, which carries the allergy-inducing saliva that causes asthma in those who suffer from that beastly affliction; and with a sinking heart I realise that this, and the complication of Snowy, their dog, who is also allergic to cats as well as hating them, are likely to fuse together to keep them away in future. However, in spite of so unpromising a start, Margot, David and I climb up to the top of the crags, and in spite of the cold greyness of this November weekend, the views across the fells, in one direction towards the Yorkshire peaks and in the other toward the Lakeland mountains, is breathtaking and awe-inspiring and I am gratified by their enthusiasms. Michael and Laurence disappear together to do some shopping, although it emerges later that this entailed going into a bar some-where that coincidentally was showing a football match

that involved Blackburn Rovers, so no greater love hath Laurence, as the Arsenal supporter that he is.

The following morning, after breakfast, Laurence also climbs the crags with his father, and as this day is a glorious clear sharp frosty day, they have the benefit of those really far-reaching dark blue and mauve views of the big distance. Shortly after this, when we are talking of breakfast-related things, they make me collapse with laughter as David recalls:

'Do you remember that morning, Laurence, which might possibly have been the happiest day of your childhood, when you opened your packet of Cocopops and out fell not just one, not just two, but a whole string of those plastic trophies you were collecting?' Laurence grins widely, but then replies somewhat lugubriously:

'Yup, they really messed up. It wasn't just a few; it was a whole plastic run of them, hundreds – hardly any Cocopops, but a whole cereal box of plastic tat! The only trouble was it did include an awful lot of duplicates, so I still had real trouble collecting a set. In fact, I never did get a complete set together.'

Geoffrey comes across for lunch too as it is a long while since he last saw Margot, David and Laurence, and in the early afternoon Michael and I wave them all goodbye. As we watch them drive down the road I say a prayer to St Joseph that this completes the proper acknowledgement of The Old Coach House as our new home, because now much of Michael's family has seen it and some of mine, and surely that will mean that we are allowed to stay here and start our new life with possibly even a small new feline family?

The following day we are told by our estate agent that a lady who had viewed Moon Cottage, and on whom we were counting, said she wanted to live on a quieter road. Two days later I get an email from Margot, which helps me to know, in spite of the difficulties with Moon Cottage, that we are in the right place:

From:	Margot
To:	Marilyn
Sent:	Tuesday, 30 November, 21:35
Subject:	Thank you – late, sorry!

Dear Marilyn and Michael
   Thank you for a really lovely weekend. Your house is wonderful and I do so hope that it all works out and you get a buyer for Moon Cottage.
   Love Margot

And shortly after we get this email we hear from another agent that there is someone else interested in the cottage. She saw it on Monday and loved it. So yet again everything remains up in the air, but we are well and we have each other, which is what counts. We wobble a little sometimes, oh yes, we wobble, but what's a wobble here and there?

ACKNOWLEDGEMENTS

The following people in some way contributed to the writing of this book and I am much indebted to them:

Sue Baker; Jean and Steve Beaman; Hilary and Catherine Bull; Charles Carroll; Annabel and Richard Challenor; Alan and Valerie Clarke; Kate Cooper; Judy, Rod and Mark Cotton; Linda Crosby; Rob Davies; Barry Delves; Elspeth Dougall; Maarit Drachman; Margot Edwards; Janet and Peter Freeman; Julie Hatherall; Padraig Healey; Jeff, Karen, Lesley, Neil and Alex Hilton; Katrina Huntley; Marje and Ian Klokow; Patrick Knowles; Judith Longman; Jacqueline Miller;

Geoffrey Moorhouse; Clive Norman; Richard Peters; Doreen and Thomas Raw; Iain and Judith Robertson; Ian and Elizabeth Rooke; Karin Scherer; Louise Sherwin-Stark; Karin Slaughter; Andy Sparkes; Pamela Stewart-Pearson; Janice Swanson; Lisa Tardioli; Robert and Louise Topping; Peter Warner; Jean Whitnall; Shirley and Stephen Windmill; Gerard Winnard; Jo Yardley; and assorted members of the Dugdale clan, including Damian, Jo and Oskar, Father John, Johnathan, Oliver and especially dear Michael.

I would also like to thank the entire staff of Hodder & Stoughton, Bookpoint and Curtis Brown, and the many staff of the following chains who so magnificently supported and believed in the earlier books:

Ottakar's; Waterstones; Borders and Books Etc; Amazon; WH Smith; and those wonderful independents all around the country together with their supporting wholesalers.

For Information on the Cats, the Author and the Illustrator

Website: http://www.thecatsofmooncottage.co.uk
Email: Mooncottagecats@hotmail.com
Post: The Old Coach House
          Hutton Roof
          Kirkby Lonsdale
          Cumbria
          LA6 2PG
          United Kingdom

I have been delighted and very moved by the many cat stories from readers all around the world, and I promise I will continue to do my best to answer you all.

Animal **Health** Trust

A percentage of all author royalties are sent to the Animal Health Trust as a contribution towards promoting feline welfare.

Registered Charity 209642

The Feline Unit at the Animal Health Trust

Cats are now the most popular domestic pet in the United Kingdom. From a veterinary perspective cats are notably different from dogs, and suffer from some very different diseases. Unfortunately our level of understanding is still relatively poor for many feline disease conditions. The Animal Health Trust is an internationally renowned centre of excellence that seeks to improve the health and welfare of animals by studying the

337

diseases that affect them, so that better diagnosis, treatment, control and prevention can be achieved. The Feline Unit within the Animal Health Trust's Small Animal Hospital is dedicated to promoting feline welfare by providing the highest quality of care for sick cats, and by contributing to studies that are concerned with broader aspects of feline health and welfare that can impact on the quality of life of all cats. Among the diseases that are currently being investigated at the Feline Unit are feline asthma and feline arthritis. It is hoped a better understanding will lead to improved diagnosis and treatment of these common conditions.

The contact details for the Feline Unit at the Animal Health Trust are:

Lanwades Park, Kentford, Newmarket, Suffolk, CB8 7UU, United Kingdom
Tel: (+44) 8700 502424
Fax: (+44) 8700 502425

Dr Andy Sparkes, BvetMed, PhD, DipECVIM, MRCVS, RCVS